The Asperger Personal Guide

Raising self-esteem and making the most of yourself as an adult with Asperger's syndrome

Genevieve Edmonds and Dean Worton

P·C·P
Paul Chapman
Publishing

Paul Chapman Publishing
A SAGE Publications Company
1 Oliver's Yard
55 City Road
London EC1Y 1SP

SAGE Publications Inc.
2455 Teller Road
Thousand Oaks, California 91320

SAGE Publications India Pvt Ltd
B-42, Panchsheel Enclave
Post Box 4109
New Delhi 110 017

www.luckyduck.co.uk

Commissioning Editor: Barbara Maines
Editorial Team: Wendy Ogden, Sarah Lynch, Mel Maines
Designer: Nick Shearn
Photographs: Andrew Bailey

A catalogue record for this book is available from the British Library

Library of Congress Control Number 2006901495

ISBN 13 978-1-4129-2257-9 (pbk)   ISBN 10 1-4129-2257-7 (pbk)

Printed on paper from sustainable resources
Printed in Great Britain by The Cromwell Press Ltd, Trowbridge, Wiltshire

About the authors

Genevieve Edmonds is a 25 year old with 'residual' Asperger's syndrome, which she views as a significant gift. She works as an associate of the Missing Link Support Service Ltd. in Lancashire, supporting those 'disabled by society' including individuals with ASD. She speaks and writes frequently in the field of Autism, along with giving training, workshops and soon counselling. She aims to empower those with ASD, carers and professionals in the understanding of Asperger's syndrome as a difference rather than an impairment. She lives and works in a solution-focused way and is based in north-west England.

Dean Worton is a 33 year old high functioning individual with a very positive expression of Asperger syndrome. He runs a successful UK-based website for adults with Asperger's syndrome and hosts real life meet-ups around the UK for its members. His key interest is in encouraging adults to live positively and successfully with the gifts that Asperger's syndrome provides. He also works in administration and resides in north-west England.

Dedications

Genevieve: To Gracie, Dan and all the horses I have ever loved.

Acknowledgements

Again to Luke Beardon for doing not one but three excellent forewords; same to Andrew for photography. Also to Vicky, Mike, Giles, Mark, Mand and Judy for your rich and insightful case studies.

Contents

Foreword

In the *Asperger Personal Guide* Gen and Dean have tackled many of the very real issues faced on a daily basis by countless individuals with Asperger's syndrome (AS). They have done so in an insightful, supportive manner that should provide heightened awareness for any parent, professional, or carer, as well as for the most important group of all – individuals with AS.

It is often said that 'honesty is the best policy'. Gen and Dean have been bluntly honest in their text, and all readers should consider carefully what they are saying. Although the majority of people would agree that being honest is a noble and positive trait, so rarely are people with AS treated with genuine honesty and respect for their way of thinking. Misunderstandings begin with non-diagnosis and misdiagnosis. Individuals with AS may have a sense that they are somehow worth less than the neurologically typical (NT) population. So often this leads to a low self-esteem, depression, anxiety and other secondary psychiatric problems. Many of the problems encountered by people with AS can be exacerbated when NT people fail to understand and demonstrate detrimental attitudes. Conversely, the honesty of the individual with AS is often seen as inappropriate, lacking in social convention and niceties.

It has happened often in my career that I have met undiagnosed AS children in education. These individuals have labels such 'naughty child', 'arrogant', 'selfish', 'spoilt', 'offensive', 'non-compliant', 'self-centred'. Sometimes they are seen as deliberately obtuse when they behave in ways which are different from others. In actual fact, when seen from an AS perspective, it is highly likely that these 'behaviours' are a direct result of the individual being honest and assuming that what is said to them is equally honest. In reply to the question by the teacher, 'Do you think you know better than me?' the honest answer "Yes" is taken as cheeky or rude. The instruction, 'Write down what you did during the weekend,' can lead to pages and pages of detailed information, only to get the response, "Well, it was obvious what I meant, the child is being deliberately annoying." Even when diagnosed it is often difficult to explain how chaotic and trying the NT world actually is for the individual with AS.

I have such unlimited admiration for people with AS who manage to co-exist alongside the NT population without being driven to despair by NT illogic and refusal to accept an AS way of thinking. Many NTs are

1

so ingrained in being NT that it is often the automatic assumption that everyone should follow the same rules, have the same understanding. "Look at me when I'm talking to you" is a classic phrase, so often used without understanding that making eye contact and listening to the speaker are incompatible activities for most people with AS.

Frustratingly, it does not take a huge effort to alter one's own cognitive process to take into account a different way of thinking – and once this has been accomplished, the positive results for people with AS are limitless. Rather than expecting everyone to be the same (how boring) diversity should be celebrated and supported. Rather than assuming that the NT way is the only way, or even the best way, we should be recognising – as Gen and Dean do in this text – some of the extremely positive 'traits' often found in individuals with AS, and including the AS population into the NT world as equal partners. The latter part of the book, which looks at the very positive qualities found in many individuals with AS, is a sobering reminder of how small changes in NT thinking could have a profound and positive impact on the lives of people with AS.

It is noted in the text (page 37) that 'unreasonable people cannot be reasoned with'. It is a delightful phrase that has a huge impact on the way in which individuals with AS have to live their lives. Perhaps it is true. However, I suspect that most NTs would willingly be reasoned with – if they only realised in the first instance how much an impact they had over the lives of people with AS. Much of the distress caused by NTs to individuals with AS is not done deliberately but rather out of ignorance and a lack of understanding and would be greatly reduced with an increase in understanding and acceptance of diverse ways of thinking and differing cognitive processes. It is thus with great enthusiasm that I am able to introduce this text. Not only will it provide valuable support and help for people with AS, it should also provide a greater insight into the lives of people with AS to the NT population.

It is, once again, with gratitude and respect that I thank Gen and Dean for their wonderful insight and hard work in writing this book, and it is with great hope that with their help, and with the help of their AS peers, the NT population will continue to make adjustments and changes to better support and accommodate people with AS.

Luke Beardon

Senior Lecturer in Autism, Sheffield Hallam University

Introduction

So you get a late diagnosis of Asperger's syndrome as an adult or suspect that you have Asperger's syndrome. You may have been lucky enough to get a diagnosis pre-adulthood and may have received support. You get to 18, whatever your circumstances, and you are left wondering, what next? At present, in terms of support and understanding for adult Aspies, the answer is very little. As far as is known, autism is a life long condition, yet where is there consistent life-long provision for Asperger's adults? This means real, not token, provision provided with an understanding that AS adults, despite their outward appearance and intelligence need consistent, timely and appropriate support often right across many aspects of their lives. Yet, is Asperger's syndrome itself really the disorder, or is the disorder a society that refuses to accept or respect difference?

Society must take responsibility for the real needs of this group, in the knowledge that to make a difference to the lives of these individuals with enormous potential, it must begin to embrace its moral obligations for inclusion – true social inclusion. There is often too much emphasis placed on the 'severity' of a person's autism, meaning that the needs of Asperger's individuals are often ignored due to having a 'mild' form of autism. Rather a more 'needs led' structure would be preferable since having an average to above average intelligence, often fluent language skills and a more invisible expression of a disability merits complex support needs of its own.

This third guide, in a series of three introductory self-help practical life guides for adults with Asperger's syndrome, aims to cover some of the personal issues that an adult with AS faces in a world not designed for people with autism. These issues are often related to mental and physical wellbeing. Anyone can have mental health problems, yet unsurprisingly for adults with AS these problems are all too common. This guide aims to provide strategies and advice for gaining self-esteem and emotional wellbeing in a society where Asperger's syndrome is seen as a 'disability', 'impairment' and yet is not supported. Whilst society 'gets its act together' to acknowledge these needs and provide appropriate support, however long that has to take, AS individuals are here, alive and kicking, trying to live everyday lives – some struggling through with some success, others with none. Therefore this guide provides some solutions that may help an individual to help themselves

NB: The advice given in this guide is based on personal experiences and is a reflection only of personal opinion. Some of the perspectives given within the guide will not be shared by everyone involved in the world of autism. There are no right and wrong answers, since everyone on the autistic spectrum is undoubtedly an individual. The guide is designed to put forward ideas and opinions from which individuals can take as much or as little as they choose. It is written to be used as a starting point, as an exercise from which further thinking is encouraged. It is not designed as a set of theories, which dictate the needs or ideas of people with Asperger's syndrome as a whole.

A note on terminology used in this guide

Aspie – This refers to an able high-functioning individual with Asperger's syndrome. However, the book can be used by lower functioning individuals on the autistic spectrum with support from a support worker, carer, parent or trusted friend.

NTs – a term used for the purposes of writing referring to mainstream neurologically 'normal' (neurotypical) individuals.

AS – short for Asperger's syndrome.

ASD – short for Autistic Spectrum Disorder.

Autistic – covering people on the whole autistic spectrum including people with Asperger's syndrome, High Functioning Autism and Classic Autism.

Chapter 1

Asperger's syndrome in adulthood
the reality

This guide aims to support the concept that adults with Asperger's syndrome can have happy and rewarding lives. It seems that it is partly an issue of training your mind. How often does it feel like you are receiving constant 'blows' when you are trying to do things which seem to come easily to everyone else? How often do you experience the frustration, and it can at the time make you think, 'Why bother, I've tried a few times and I still keep getting it wrong. I'll never get it right.' However, this is where the word perseverance comes in. For example, some people pass their driving test on the eighth attempt, and a salesman may have been turned down at every single house in a street and is at the only house that he has not yet tried and actually makes a sale. Life is funny like that, so it is worth trying something many times if you want it badly enough and never giving up. One of the lovely things about many Aspies is their tenacity and strength to keep going, a stubbornness to not give up. Thank goodness many Aspies have this strength.

Some of the deficits of Asperger's syndrome are mostly only thought as so by a majority, perhaps people who do not know any better. It's a tired old fact that anything not practiced by the majority is bound to be considered odd. However, this does not mean it is necessarily wrong, it is just that people do not understand it. It is fear of the unknown and this tends too often to make life a misery for Aspies just for not blending in. It seems sometimes that having an invisible social 'disability' can be one of the cruellest hands to be dealt. The general social world is one where fitting in, in terms of behaviour, is the goal for happiness, deviating from this is to be an individual and this is seen as negative.

However, there are, in reality, many benefits of having Asperger's syndrome. Asperger's syndrome can be thought of as a gift of which to be proud and cherish. After all if you follow the crowd and copy all the social habits of the majority you would be a clone and not an individual. The world needs individuals, without which the world would be a very boring place indeed. However, it doesn't seem possible to change the ingrained nature of the majority overnight, or over many days and nights for that matter! It seems that in the meantime, one key for happiness and survival as an AS adult might be to play the game enough to meet your individually chosen needs. One individual's chosen needs may mean that they have to try and completely change themselves to fit in. Others may be independent enough to need very little from the social world.

We've all heard the news; many famous influential people have/had/are suspected to have/had autistic traits. This is indeed good to hear, but how does this translate to the everyday folk with Asperger's syndrome, the run-of-the-mill people with AS trying to get by? Aspies do indeed quite often have unique skills, but that doesn't necessarily mean that every Aspie is going to be the next great scientist, composer or artist. However, despite many Aspies finding difficulty in several areas which most people tend not to, a number of Aspies are talented in a few specific areas and often put those without AS to shame in these areas. This means that Aspies can be indispensable in the company they work for or perhaps in a chance encounter. The idea is to capitalise as much as possible on these abilities whilst coping with the difference they bring. This is all about individual goals, whatever they may be.

Debating whether Asperger's syndrome is really a disability

The current thinking that Asperger's syndrome is not actually a disability in the same way that having a physical or sensory impairment such as being paralysed or blind may be seen is indeed helpful. However, what is far more difficult to define is what makes it become a disability. It seems to only become a problem because of the expectations that are placed on members of society, within their communities and the everyday social world. One reason that people with Asperger's syndrome have problems with things that the majority of people they know don't seem to have is because their mind is wired slightly differently, and this means that they think in a different way to that of the majority of the population. It is hardly surprising when say, for argument's sake, 90% of the population do things a certain way, that the remaining 10% will appear unusual and will often be deemed to have done something wrong. So is it therefore just an issue of minority figures? You happen to be in a minority, so you become disabled for the rest of your life?

Not doing as the majority does, does not equate to accepting a 'disabled' status. It may be more a case of the majority being locked into the mindset that if nearly everyone else does something a certain way then that is the way to do it.

This may all sound very obvious to some readers or not so obvious to others. It is important to remember that in theory it seems straightforward to look at Asperger's syndrome as a 'minority way of being' or a 'different culture', but in the majority world the task of helping others to see this is a mammoth and tiring task. It is unsurprising that the mental health and wellbeing of Asperger's individuals in an non-accepting environment will suffer.

It is, however, also extremely encouraging that there are examples of Asperger's individuals whose AS virtually disappears as a 'disorder' if surrounded by the right people in an environment that works for them.

One of the main criteria for being diagnosed with Asperger's syndrome is having difficulties with social interactions. In many ways this may be simply because there are unspoken social rules which are supposed to be observed, which people with Asperger's syndrome are unaware of or perhaps do not see as so important. This does not necessarily mean that the person with Asperger's syndrome is being rude. It may just be that they have a different way of doing things, which is not necessarily wrong but many people would consider it to be wrong or at the very least odd, purely because it differs from what they are used to.

Therefore, it is perfectly feasible that in many cases, the difficulties of people with Asperger's syndrome are caused by people not understanding anything that is slightly different from the norm and finding fault with it, instead of thinking that it is creative thinking and refreshing that not everyone thinks exactly the same.

Culture has a lot to do with the level of perception of difficulty for a person with Asperger's syndrome. In majority culture, it can be very difficult for people with Asperger's syndrome in some social situations due to expectations that people should show confidence and do everything to a certain standard. However, there are some countries or areas within countries in the world where the pace of life is slower and people are not expected to live up to this expectation. It may be that in these places a person may be seen as an individual and accepted the way they are; or perhaps the interests or emphasis in the area are less on social priorities or social conformity. It would be nice to think that this would leave the person with AS the chance to live just as good a life as their fellow nationals. However, when culture is discussed in this context it is not suggesting that someone who has been diagnosed with AS and has problems would have to move to a different country or continent to avoid the problems. Culture can vary so much within one country or part of a country, or even within a town or village.

The following are two different scenarios. Both scenarios involve people with Asperger's syndrome. They are identical twins being raised apart, one by the mother and stepfather, the other by the father and stepmother. They both have the same level of IQ and similar cognitive traits and personalities, but, perhaps due to their different circumstances, seem completely different to each other in just about every way.

Scenario one

John was brought up by his mother and stepfather. They were not very accepting of his differences and were always very critical of him, always having focused on the negative points. He was rarely praised for things that he did well, and he was always very negative about himself. He was extremely shy and anxious and did not join in with the activities of others. Other children, including his stepbrothers, always found him very odd because he always either withdrew completely or made awkward social approaches, which lead to him being laughed at and ridiculed. This lead to some severe bullying and he was afraid to go to school on his own. Due to this his mother drove him to school but complained about doing so, something which John found very stressful. His stepfather has never been accepting of John. He feels that John is a very weak individual and every day calls him a 'wimp'. His mother has never conveyed a very caring attitude as she feels that John's behaviour is pathetic and as she always reminds him. He feels that he is a huge disappointment to his mother because he is not the type of son she wanted. It is very depressing for John that he feels unable to turn to his mother to talk about his worries. He feels completely alone in the world. He has always been a loner and rarely had friends because at school and in the neighbourhood he stood out as being 'weird' and often called a 'freak'. He has, in the past, been friends with other quiet people or people whom appeared to have a warm demeanour but all of these friendships have been very short-lived and these friends have soon appeared to favour the company of others.

He has never understood why he is so different. He has always wanted to fit in but feels that he just can't because every time he has tried it just never seems to work. Therefore, he simply does not make an effort socially and withdraws, spending most of his time in his bedroom. He has an obsession with tractors and used to talk endlessly about them until he was told to 'shut up', having not taken the hint that no one was interested. If he ever does leave his bedroom he goes to a nearby farm where he knows there is a tractor and he sits himself down next to the tractor. He has received a lot of teasing due to his obsession about tractors, as unfortunately most people cannot understand how someone can have such an interest. He spends time alone in his room making a scrapbook full of pictures of tractors out of farming magazines. Nowadays he does not tell anyone about his obsession but as a child, while his peer group played games, he spent his time daydreaming about tractors, and withdrew entirely from other people. Sometimes he goes for several days not uttering a single word to other people. He has a fairly good relationship with his grandparents and sometimes as a child they took him out at the weekends, but even then he would sometimes go for over two hours without speaking a single word, and if relatives were visiting the house, he went up to his room.

He used computers at school, but never really understood them. Whenever he tried using a computer unaided something went wrong, and he couldn't work out how to put it right. He would just sit there until the teacher eventually got around to him and saw that he was having difficulties. The teacher would simply fix the problem and walk away. John did not know what the teacher had done, and was fearful of touching any of the other buttons in case something else rendered him helpless for another fifteen minutes. Therefore, he now makes no effort to try to understand computers and avoids them like the plague. He has no confidence in his ability to do anything. If he does something well, he does not see that this may be a hidden talent, he just assumes that it must be beginners luck, as he does not believe that he could possibly be good at anything. Therefore he does not even try. If he ever has the opportunity to try something new he always declines as he does not see the point. His outlook is that if you don't try something you can't be disappointed when it doesn't work out. He also won't accept help when it is offered and simply festers and allows himself to get into difficulties over things which he might be able to do quite well if he could just be helped. If he is ever asked a question about something he instantly answers with the words, 'I don't know,' even though quite often he does know the answer. He doesn't think for a few seconds to come up with the answer because he doesn't expect to be able to come up with the answer and so doesn't even try. He allows misunderstandings to spiral out of control. At times when someone would cease to be angry with him if he simply communicated a particular fact he says nothing, as he is too afraid to speak out. He also takes what people say to him very literally and takes things to heart even when it is said as a joke and the person was trying to be friendly.

He is now in his mid-twenties but lives a very solitary existence. He has recently moved out of his mother's house. He was never happy there but he could not have easily afforded to live anywhere else. He made no effort in his exams at school, although still did well enough to go to university. At first, he did not apply to go to university because he did not think that his grades would be good enough. He was puzzled that he received high grades as he had convinced himself that he was going to fail. He did find some confidence to apply to university the next year. He is completely terrified at the prospect of going to university. He had applied to live in the Halls of Residence on his campus because he was scared at the prospect of having to contact letting agents and look round houses with them. He had been going to move into the Halls the day before he was due to enroll, but he lost his nerve and did neither. He had made up his mind that he was not going to go to university because the whole idea was too bewildering, but he was depressed for the next two weeks and thought long and hard about whether he had made the right decision. He could not settle and started his university course a week late, which meant that he missed the first week of classes and missed out on getting to know other students on his course. Students in the Halls had also made friends already, and because he was so awkward and nervous around the other students both at university and in the Halls, people seemed to give him a wide berth. People said 'hello' to him but he reacted very awkwardly and people often interpreted this as rudeness or being stuck-up. Having not arrived in the first week, he missed the Fresher's fair and so did not find out about clubs and societies at the university. Due to his obsessive interest in tractors, he might have enjoyed being a member of the university Agricultural Society, but as he did not go to the Fresher's fair, he did not even know that the Agricultural Society existed.

He soon caught up despite missing the first week and his marks were good, but as times got on he found it harder to concentrate on his work because he never had any company and this began to trouble him. He had thought that at university he would be able to fit in somewhere, but he had made no connections with anyone on his course or in the Halls. Any attempts that had ever been made at being friendly with him tended to be reciprocated so awkwardly that sometimes people would reply with, 'Don't speak then.' This was very distressing for John because he so desperately wanted to have friends but he felt that he was marring any potential opportunities with his social awkwardness. John felt so lonely and unable to concentrate on his work that when he returned home during his Easter holidays he did not go back to university. His teachers were very disappointed because they thought that he was such an able student with the potential to get a very good degree and a very good career.

John was depressed for several months afterwards, but eventually found some motivation to look for employment as he did not want to spend the rest of his life alone in his bedroom looking at magazines about tractors. He had a number of interviews, but did not come across very well at interview. He never made eye contact, spoke in a monotone and didn't smile. In some cases, the employer decided to give him a chance due to his good qualifications, but John was always unsure of his abilities and did not mix well with his colleagues. On each occasion, his contract was terminated within a very short space of time and he never fully understood why the job had ended or if he did understand, why they had never discussed this with him prior to making the decision to end the contract. Again, this made him feel very negative about himself. At one job, he did actually make a very good friend who had managed to connect with him and saw something in John that other people didn't. This friend took John to places that he had never been to before and for once John was happy. This was the best friend that John had ever had in his life, but John felt that as the job had ended that he could not continue with the friendship, and he severed all ties with his new friend.

John has taken various training courses but never speaks to any of the other attendees. He only ever leaves the house to attend these courses and to visit his local job centre to search for employment. He spends his time sitting at home either watching television or in his room adding to his scrapbooks of tractor pictures. He never goes out, and his mother and stepfather are still very unsupportive. He has no social life whatsoever and has never been in a relationship or even had an encounter with a member of the opposite sex. This has made him very depressed, and he has now started to look through library books trying to see if he can identify what has made him this way. He saw an article about Asperger's syndrome, and feels that it applies to him. He is now just trying to summon up the courage to broach the topic with his doctor.

Scenario two

David is Johns' identical twin. They were separated from each other when they were three years old. Before this, David and John did all of the same things at the same time, and had the same personalities as each other. It was impossible to tell any differences between the two, and their mother was the only person who could tell them apart. You've read about John; now read David's story and notice where their behaviours became completely different from each other.

David was brought up by his father and stepmother. They always wanted the best for David and because of his differences thought that he was a very special child and possibly a genius. He was always praised for things that he did well, felt very loved and was a very happy child. When other children played games at first he felt quite anxious and confused about joining in, but he always eventually found the courage, and usually took part in their activities even if he was on the outside of the group as an observer. Other children found him to be smiley and cheerful, he was well-liked and liked helping people, despite seeming different socially and rather eccentric. On the few occasions that anyone did try to bully him, he tried to defend himself. From when he started Junior School, he would always either walk to school on his own or with other children when he could manage it. His stepmother is very accepting of David and has always loved him as though he was her own. She always noticed that something was different about him but never saw this as a problem, and loved the fact that he was so individual. She feels that David has a lot of unique qualities and every day when he was younger called him 'special'. His father has always conveyed a very caring attitude and feels that David is a 'unique gift' as he always keeps reminding him. David feels very self-assured knowing that his parents are both so proud of him. It really helps him to know that every time he feels upset about anything he can go to his father and tell him how he feels, and he knows that he will always help him to feel better. He feels supported. Despite not having lots of friends at school or in the neighbourhood, he stands out as being a well-liked kid and sometimes he was even described by other children as being 'cool' whilst others continue to bully him. Some of the more open-minded children seemed to respect his unconventional and quirky ways, perhaps as David likes himself as he is. He befriended some quiet children and remained a loyal friend to them and helped them to boost their confidence.

He has always known that there is something different about him compared with other children, but he is really pleased to not be like everyone else as he feels the world would be a boring place if there were no 'individuals'. He feels that too many people are like clones of one another and just follow each other around as if they are sheep. He has never needed to try to make friends as friendship always seems to look for him, and when it hasn't he is happy alone. He has been invited to parties and been to many of these, dancing and enjoying himself despite not being that keen on them. Still, he does not want to be friends with everyone, favouring the company of quieter, thinking people, who he feels are more on his wavelength. Although he is outgoing himself, he feels happiest around quieter people and finds them more interesting to be around.

The one thing that would perhaps mark David out the most as being different is his interest in tractors. He has posters up in his living room, and always enjoyed being around tractors and riding them when this had been arranged with the farmer. Like John, he also used to have scrapbooks full of pictures of tractors. He recalls one occasion when he spoke at length to his father and stepmother about his interest in tractors, but found out that they weren't really very interested in the subject. They told him this in a straightforward and helpful way to help David learn social skills rather than making him feel deficient. He has not tried to share his interest again to such a degree, as he learnt that it is something that not many people would want to know all about. However, whenever they were passing by a farm, David's father would look out for either the farmer or another member of the farm staff. He would always attempt to create a conversation with them and mention David's interest in tractors. Sometimes David was able to have a ride in the tractor. He would ask the farmer lots of questions about the tractor, and usually the farmer didn't seem to mind. David was a very happy child, but was never happier than when he was around tractors. This helped him build some social confidence.

Only a couple of David's friends know about his interest in tractors and they have never ridiculed him about it, but he hasn't mentioned it to anyone else. Although tractors are his specialist interest, it is not his only hobby. Like many people with Asperger's syndrome he also collects maps. He enjoys playing musical instruments and has found that he is very gifted at this. Although he spends most of his time with his quieter friends, he still exchanges pleasantries with more outgoing people, even though he is not always so keen on a lot of the small talk that goes along with this. He has a good relationship with his grandparents and when he was younger they really doted on him. He tries to be chatty with others, such as relatives, for as long as he can manage it despite finding it tiring. He makes time to play with any relatives' visiting children, despite finding it difficult. They think he is a lot of fun, and have all stated that David is their favourite uncle.

When David first used a computer at school, he found it very confusing to work out how to use it, even though he did ask the teacher what exactly it was that he was supposed to be doing. However, he remembered the advice of his parents that some things take a bit more getting used to than others, so he would remain patient during his first few flawed attempts at using computers, and persevere. Eventually it all fell into place, and he gradually became very good at using computers. As an adult he has a real talent for using them, and teaches adults how to use computers at night classes in his local college. David has found many things difficult when he has been unused to doing them but has always followed the exact same principles as he did for using computers. He has found that he has far more of an aptitude for doing a lot of manual things than he ever imagined he would be able to. He deals with all the little jobs that need doing around his house, except for when he is legally obliged to call out a qualified electrician. He completely re-decorated his home when he moved in as it needed a lot of work doing to it. In doing this, he has managed to increase the value of his house. Whenever David does something well, he explores this ability to see if it can be made useful in some way, and has even made a bit of extra money, without breaking the law, by using some of his skills. His outlook is that if you don't try you'll never know what joys are waiting around the next corner despite the anxiety it can cause. He is constantly amazed at how many things he can do well and also finds enjoyable. Sometimes, because of his Asperger's syndrome (which is undiagnosed), there are things that David has difficulty understanding and he misinterprets something. However, he always talks through the problem and the person with whom the misunderstanding took place usually realises that David had not meant to be offensive and the matter is quickly resolved. David rarely takes anything literally now, despite doing so when he was younger. If something sounds a bit implausible he tends to think it through and realise that what the person said was unlikely. David is very easy-going and never takes anything that is said about him to heart. He tends to politely ask the person what they meant by what they said, and if it turns out they were being friendly this can sometimes lead to friendships. The way he sees it is that if the person was attempting to make a joke, he is fine with that, and if they were genuinely making an offensive remark, he pities that person and doesn't see the point of getting upset about it. He has enough respect for himself not to spend time worrying about people who have some irrational reason for not having respect for him.

He was reluctant to leave home because he has always had such a good relationship with his father and stepmother, and had such happy times living there. He worked very hard at school and did well. His father and stepmother wanted him to study towards becoming a lawyer, because of his high level of intelligence, but due to his social difficulties he was realistic in accepting that this would not be a good career for him. He went to the same university as his long-lost identical twin brother John. However, not only did he actually find out about the Agricultural society and join it, but he also took a degree in Agricultural Engineering. He thoroughly enjoyed writing up his dissertation because for this he had chosen to write a comparison between the safety requirements for different types of tractors. He even found out lots of things about tractors that he never knew and that his brother John would never find out.

David had applied to live in Halls of Residence and was accepted, but two weeks before enrolment he decided that he would prefer to live in a shared student house as this would mean that he could have some peace and quiet to get on with his studies. David accepted all invitations to social events or just general visits to the Student Union bar, though often only stayed for about an hour or two. He occasionally went to nightclubs with fellow students but not too often because he took his studies seriously. He enjoyed going to different parts of the city looking at different houses and meeting lots of different interesting potential housemates. He eventually moved into a pleasant quiet area, got on well with his fellow housemates and was invited out to the pub with them. He also got on really well with people from his degree course and the Agricultural Society as he found it easier to socialise around a shared interest. Although he had always superficially got on well with most of his peers, he felt that there was something really amazing about spending time with so many others who shared his interest in Agricultural Engineering.

David was in his element when he went to the Fresher's fair and there was a stall for an Agricultural Society. He takes part in that every Wednesday afternoon, and each week they go to a different farm and afterwards to a country pub to sit down and talk about the afternoon's events. David has very fond memories of sitting in a nice, quiet country pub by a lovely, warm log fire talking about farming with other people of his age. Before he went to university, he never thought he would meet another young person as interested in farming as he was, and yet here were over a dozen other young people sharing his interest.

When David completed his university education, he had some difficulty getting a job in a firm of Agricultural Engineers. He didn't come across very well at the first few interviews he attended and became despondent. However, his self-belief and tenacity spurred him to keep trying. Thankfully, one company was able to look at the strengths he showed on his CV and the potential he showed as an employee rather than focusing on the socially unusual ways he behaved. David found the job really interesting and showed great commitment. Some colleagues found him difficult to work with and hard to communicate with. He had learnt throughout his life to focus on his strengths, which tended to be accuracy, knowledge, focus and being helpful to others. David also writes the weekly tractor column in a magazine about agriculture and has written some very entertaining and lively articles about tractors.

After he finished working in the Agricultural Engineering company where he had his first job, David still kept in touch with his colleagues and regularly went out for a drink or a meal with them. On one occasion, one of his colleagues brought his sister along. She was very interested to hear about tractors, even though she knew nothing about them herself. Although David, who was by this time twenty-three years old, had had many friends, he had never had a girlfriend before. Elizabeth became David's first girlfriend and is now his partner.

Although David does have Asperger's syndrome and has found difficulties in certain aspects of his life, these have never been sufficient enough for him to really give any thought to the fact that anything could be wrong with him. He is none the wiser that he has a mild form of autism, and he has never even heard of Asperger's syndrome.

Comparing the two scenarios

As you will notice, these two men have totally different outlooks on life and you would be very hard pressed to find anything that they have in common personality wise. However, in the first three years of their lives they both grew up together, were inseparable and did everything the same way. John's problems are very obvious, and it seems that he will have no difficulty convincing his doctor that he has Asperger's syndrome. However, if David had ever heard of Asperger's syndrome, he would be unlikely to think that he was affected by it, and it will be very hard for him to convince a doctor of this fact.

Here, we are demonstrating that two people with the same mindset as each other were separated from each other. At first they reacted in the same way to losing their identical twin, but eventually started to develop different characteristics from each other. The evidence suggests that part of the reason for this is because they were brought up in entirely different environments with different support. David was loved and nurtured and always encouraged to make the best of himself, despite his apparent difficulties. He was taught at an early age how to overcome problems quickly. His differences others were praised whereas John's behaviour attracted negative responses. As you would imagine from their identical characteristics as young children, John is as equally gifted as David, but this is not picked up on and supported. Perhaps if John had been treated with greater respect, he might have had a more fulfilled life and his difference might not have been so obvious.

The fact that David actually made a career out of his own interest in tractors even though that was only one of his interests and John, who is still obsessed with tractors, never even thought to turn this into a career, points perhaps to how the different experiences that they had have impacted on them both. It has made one of them excessively negative and depressed whilst the other has a fairly happy, successful life despite the problems.

The fact that David manages pretty well in life perhaps points to the fact that John is not really the lost cause that people may seem to think he is.

His problems are not necessarily of his own creating but are perhaps the creation of ignorance and unhelpful support. People will be all too ready to judge John and to have him down as less able than he really is. Using David as an example, it is not hard to tell that John does not really have all the problems that he has been labelled with. He appears to have been moulded into a very depressed person with no confidence in himself and this could potentially lead to him being classed as mentally unwell. However, David's brain appears to be wired in exactly the same way and no one would dream of classing him as mentally unwell.

As mentioned on page 8, there are some places in the world where life is more relaxed and people are given the opportunity to be just who they are.

It may be helpful to analogise the difference in cultural behaviours that already exist between countries. Where a person who is diagnosed with AS could get by fine when visiting some foreign countries, the average NT might struggle in other foreign countries, because they act in the way that they would back home and the host country might consider things that they do on a daily basis to be bizarre or even plain wrong. Perhaps it is helpful to look at Asperger's syndrome and autism as a culture of its' own?

After all, when we take into account the fact that no two countries in the world have the exact same habits and beliefs, who is to say which countries are living life the right way and which are not? A British person might say that the British way of life is the only one that makes sense, but then a French person might say that only the French really know what they're doing and an Australian that Australia is the only country that isn't clueless. They cannot possibly all be correct, so ultimately it can only be about opinion. The only situations where people can truly be said to be doing wrong is if they are breaking the law or doing something that harms an individual or themselves. Everything else is purely down to individual opinion. If a person sits on a seat in the main shopping area of their town and rocks from side to side because it calms them, most people would probably look on and think that that person is acting bizarrely. If a more socially aware individual was wanting to do this, they would likely refrain from doing it in a populated area. The thing that actually stops them from doing it is the fact that other people would be likely to assert their opinion and laugh at them and make them feel ridiculous, leading to potential bullying or exclusion. It seems silly therefore that we live in a world where we all have to adapt to the thinking style of the 'norm' in order to fit in. Unfortunately, this means that Aspies and other people on the autistic spectrum can be somewhat restricted in how they can behave. This can be very repressive in many cases, so it is not surprising if Aspies often feel depressed or that they simply don't fit in anywhere.

Often, the more socially aware an individual on the autistic spectrum is, the harder she may try to fit in, leading to a greater chance of mental distress. The compensatory effort put in can often lead to greater complications.

Should individuals, as long as they are not actually harming themselves or others, have every right to be who they are and not feel the need to hide their real selves? In practice, often depending on the country where the individual lives, to some extent characteristics of Asperger's syndrome do have to be kept under wraps in certain situations. If someone goes about something in a different way, this can be taken as being 'odd'. In some countries, children have pestered their parents to buy the latest trends each season for fear of being bullied and excluded if this does not happen. In adulthood, the expectations by society to conform are maybe not always as overt, but the fact that cultures exist in childhood where people spend so much money on fashions merely to avoid being the victims of violence proves that people can be very inflexible. The same principles can apply in several other social situations and other life situations.

John's life appears to have been entirely ruled by people rigidly imposing these expectations on him, and he really did not have a chance of happiness as he was being so severely repressed. It does not seem reasonable that John has been made so unhappy just because people were expecting him to live every single aspect of his life in a way that was clearly not right for him. Those around him did not see any alternatives, and saw him as being weak and willful when in fact he had so much to offer.

These sorts of expectations were never imposed on David, since others were able to see ways round the problems. Instead of focusing on what David could not do well, they focused on what he could do well. They discovered that he had many positive qualities, and many of these possibly would not have existed if it was not for his Asperger's syndrome.

David and John are fictional characters. If they were real individuals and we had read the two scenarios, would we have any way of knowing that the accounts were accurate? Perhaps their different life experiences were due to having different personalities; perhaps they were due to different environments; perhaps one of them had co-occuring affective problems; perhaps those around them were/weren't Asperger's friendly. We have no way of knowing, and even if we were to carry out formal research on two similar individuals would we have an accurate conclusive data about how to work out why one AS individual has had a successful life to early adulthood and the other not?

The key aim of the two scenarios is to demonstrate that two individuals fitting the diagnostic criteria for Asperger's syndrome can have very different lives. We don't need to carry out a large-scale scientifically robust study to know that each AS adult is an individual and the presentation and effects of AS are undoubtedly affected by the social factors in his life.

Chapter 2

Mental health

Please note that ideas expressed in this chapter do not have a basis in medical research or from mental health professionals. The basis is anecdotal and as such, if you have concerns over your own or another person's mental health please use the mental health contacts outlined in the back of this guide.

Mental health

Whilst inconsistent knowledge and myths continue to fly around about AS, common misconceptions still occur including the classic, 'Asperger's syndrome is a psychiatric disorder.' Asperger's syndrome is not a mental illness. In addition many people who do accept that AS is not a mental illness but a neurological difference often believe that secondary mental health problems with AS are 'par for the course' or something that should be expected or accepted. Wrong. AS does not have to occur with secondary mental health problems, yet so very often it does, especially in adulthood. With lack of appropriate understanding and support of their needs many adults become depressed, a depression which may have begun in adolescence or, even worse, in childhood.

Too many AS adults live in a state of heightened abnormal anxiety, and often experience frequent spells of mild to severe depression, which if left untreated can develop into more severe illness. At the best of times in our society, mental health issues for NTs are far too frequently ignored and 'swept under the carpet'. This doesn't leave much hope for people with AS whose mental health needs often have a very different basis than NTs. Part of the battle seems to be that many aspects of Asperger's syndrome can look like aspects of a mental illness such as schizophrenia, depression or OCD (Obsessive Compulsive Disorder). The question to ask here is does the AS person with traits which appear mentally ill want to change them? Is the AS person actually happier having rituals, obsessions or having an outlook that to others seems 'out of touch with reality'? If it makes sense to the Asperger's individual, and if it helps them cope in a world not designed for Asperger's individuals, why try to 'change' their autism if they are not harming themselves or anyone else? The key, whether it is genuine mental illness or not, is allowing the Asperger's individual to have control over how she is treated for her 'illness'.

It is important to note that it is possible for AS individuals (as much as NT individuals) to develop more severe mental illnesses such as a psychotic illness, schizophrenia or bipolar disorder (manic depression) alongside

AS. These sort of illnesses can manifest themselves in such a way that professional care is often required.

Communication issues and mental health

Due to some of the aspects of different use and interpretation of verbal and non-verbal communication in Asperger's individuals, mental health issues are frequently missed, misunderstood or ignored. Commonly, a person with Asperger's syndrome may have had mental health problems building up for some time, when a crisis occurs seemingly out of the blue. This could be due to non-verbal communication difficulties. Some Asperger's individuals are extremely hard to read by their outside presentation, meaning that they may show no signs at all of depression, appearing cheerful in their facial expression, body posture and tone of voice. Equally, there are other individuals who are more expressive but struggle to communicate how they feel and what they want despite being verbally fluent. Consequently, a number of misunderstandings can occur leading a person's needs to be over- or underestimated even by those who seem to know her well.

Getting an appointment from the mental health services is hard enough, and even when extra support is available the waiting lists can be soul-destroyingly long. As an adult with AS, ensure that you get the support you need out of the mental health services. Due to the different way you communicate and relate it may be helpful to take along an advocate or supporter who knows you well. It is too easy for AS adults to be misinterpreted in their behaviour, causing more harm than good in a mental health setting. Note down all of your concerns before you see any professionals – it is too easy to forget or struggle to get your needs across in a time-limited and pressured situation. Remember that in a formal clinical setting your behaviour may appear perfectly normal and your very real support needs may be overlooked or underestimated.

A lack of understanding of adult AS in mental health services

Adults with AS can end up in the care of the mental health services for two reasons:

1. As a person with undiagnosed Asperger's syndrome seeking help and becoming misdiagnosed as having a mental illness such as schizophrenia, bipolar disorder or a personality disorder.

23

2. As a person diagnosed (self or officially) seeking support for secondary mental health problems which are frequently brought on through lack of appropriate understanding or support for the adult's AS.

Sadly, expertise within generic mental health services for adults is very inconsistent and seemingly quite rare. This leaves a lottery situation when it comes to accessing mental health professionals with a good understanding of Asperger's syndrome in adults.

The outcome of a lack of expertise can lead to ineffective or inappropriate treatment. Such (hopefully unintentional) bad practice is not acceptable. The issues surrounding mental health problems for Asperger's adults are often different to those facing NTs with mental distress. Consequently, the outcomes for Asperger's adults are often less positive as treatment is either inappropriate or unhelpful.

Social isolation

The social isolation frequently experienced by many AS adults can lead on to mental health issues. Considering that many (not all) Asperger's adults do want to be socially involved to some degree, being socially isolated can be a crushing and deeply depressing experience. The key to coping with so many of the challenges life throws at a person seems to be centred around feeling empathy with other humans and seeking and giving support to them. A strong social network within which an individual feels a sense of belonging and is respected and welcomed will inevitably help a person navigate life's often difficult and confusing path. For many Asperger's individuals this sense of belonging, respect and feeling welcome is inconsistent and at worst non-existent. How many Asperger's individuals can actually turn to someone who really 'gets' where they are coming from? How many Asperger's individuals can easily turn to others who provide the support they are looking for?

One of the problems associated with that of social isolation is that of losing touch with social reality, or the common social existence of others. The more isolated a person becomes, the harder it becomes for a person to become integrated. So the vicious circle continues. The person may be viewed as 'odd' or a 'loner' and so attempts at social involvement are marred.

One of the strategies developed to support some Asperger's adults to avoid social isolation and exclusion is that of social groups and befriending schemes. These can work well provided the individual's level of ability and interests are met on the befriending scheme or Social Group. One of the common scenarios is that of finding appropriate level befriending. The Asperger's individual struggles in social areas but not general intelligence and so finds it more frustrating to be in a social group or with a befriender due to feeling bored, patronised or unsatisfied. It is for the individual to decide whether social isolation or social activities, which may be unsatisfying, are better. One good thing about befriending is having access to someone with a differing point of view. Although it can be frustrating being befriended by an individual who may be of equal or lower intellectual ability, sometimes spending time with anyone (within reason) is better than no one.

Depression

Depression (diagnosed or not) is worryingly common in Asperger's adults. A helpful explanation of depression is the physical and emotional effects of internalised anger or frustration. Rather than expressing anger outwardly a person will internalise their anger by bottling it up. This can eventually manifest itself in the experience of a form of depression. There is a great difference between the colloquial everyday term, 'I'm really depressed,' (denoting a person feeling a bit down for a short period) and a person who has a genuine depression. A genuine depression is not as easily controllable and may last longer, with greater intensity, than having 'the blues'.

Depression can be reactive with a clear trigger (e.g. as a direct result of a trigger such as bereavement or the loss of a relationship) which tends to be shorter-term. It can also take the form of 'endogenous' depression (coming from within, with no explainable trigger), which can be chronic and long lasting and resistant to treatment.

If you feel you or someone you know may be depressed, the signs are as follows (lasting more than two weeks to a month):

- Feeling sad, despondent and hopeless.
- Feeling guilt that's out of proportion to events.
- A loss of interest in activities previously enjoyed.
- Thinking and acting slowly.
- Under- or over-eating.
- Avoiding social contact (uncharacteristically).
- Loss of interest in sex.

- Loss of interest in appearance and self-care (more than usual).

- Irrational negative thoughts about self, others and situations.

What can be done?

- If the depression has a clear trigger (such as failing at an exam or a relationship break-up) then recovery is sometimes easier. Talking through the trigger with a friend or counsellor is helpful and identifying steps to move on from the event may do the trick. If the depression continues, seeking help from a GP may be the answer. Beware though – antidepressant medications are often given out as 'quick fixes'. Read up about the different types of antidepressant drugs before accepting any, since certain drugs do not work for everyone. Other than antidepressant drugs, some natural remedies such as St John's Wort can be helpful. For many adult Aspies the trigger for the depression is experienced on a frequent basis. The experience of having an invisible social disability and the manifestations of that such as social isolation, loneliness, un- or under-employment will be ongoing difficulties that might be associated with the depression.

- If you cannot identify a specific trigger for your depression and it seems to have 'come out if nowhere', working through it may be difficult at first.

Depression tips:

- Get moving. When depressed, a person will move less and often want to stay in bed. Whatever you do, at least try and move somehow, even if this means getting out of bed and walking or doing some basic exercise for five minutes each hour. The longer you stay still the longer your mind and body will be 'stuck' in a depressed state. Try to exercise and get fresh air. One problem with this is facing others in doing so. If you feel that you can't face the gym, swimming pool or even a walk alone, try and find someone who will support you to go, such as a befriender or support worker.

- Do something to occupy your mind, whatever that may be. Anything is better than nothing, since ruminating and worrying feeds depression.

- Don't allow yourself to withdraw totally from others. This is easier said than done for many Aspies since it is often social issues which trigger depression. However, try as much as possible to fight this avoidance behaviour, remembering that others can be a source of comfort and support – it is finding the right people that counts. If you withdraw totally from others, the chances of finding such people are reduced dramatically. Each time you find the courage to be with others during depression, praise yourself well for doing so.

- Keep your diet healthy. When depressed it is easy to eat too little or feed yourself rubbish, since that is how you feel. Make the extra effort to eat well since this will help to heal you. Concentrate on wholefoods, fresh fruit and vegetables, non-processed food, oily fish and skinless meat. Don't punish yourself with a poor diet.

- Don't turn to alcohol or drugs as a solution, the short-term effects are useless as are the long-term depressant effects that drugs and alcohol cause.

- Keep talking. Don't hold it all in. Even if it is not your natural inclination to talk – do. This can be done by email or by telephone if you can't bear face-to-face interaction (see Useful Contacts in the back of this guide).

- Try to trust those who are trying to help you.

A note on suicidal thoughts

When a person is very depressed it is not uncommon to have thoughts of suicide. There is a big difference between having these thoughts and actually having a plan for suicide. When a person gets to the point of having clear plans for how they will go about committing suicide, serious action must be taken. If this is the state you suspect you are in or someone you know is in, take immediate action. (Please see the Useful Contacts in the back of the guide.)

Why suicide?

Many individuals who want to commit suicide feel that they have exhausted all of the options available to them to cope with how they feel. They need an escape that they feel cannot be found. They need a total change from where they are. They want a solution and an end to the feelings and situation that they are in and they cannot find that in the people and environment around them.

Some people would argue that if a person wishes to take their own life they are within their rights to do so. However, it is important to remember that suicide is not the only solution, and that things can and do improve.

Anxiety

Many people with AS would agree that they suffer with above average levels of anxiety. It is accepted that anxiety is a 'key feature' of many people on the autistic spectrum. However, it is important to note whether this anxiety is in fact actually a part of the autism itself or is it as a direct result of living in a world not designed for people with autism. Some people would argue the latter.

What does anxiety feel like? You can feel or have:

- over-aroused mentally; racing thoughts
- palpitations, sweating hands, wobbly legs
- unable to concentrate
- fearfulness and apprehension
- obsessions and fixations (that are negative to the person)
- wanting to escape, hide, run away
- unable to 'think straight'
- thinking and fearing the worst
- constant worry.

What can be done about anxiety?

A lot depends on the level of anxiety a person is experiencing. If anxiety is only present in certain situations it can be more manageable. Another important point is to note that the type of anxiety experienced by NTs may be qualitatively different to that experienced by Aspies. It is very difficult to give a definitive instruction booklet for dealing with anxiety, since it is very complex. However, here are some quick tips:

- Some psychiatric drugs can be helpful for anxiety, such as tranquillizers. However, these are addictive and are not designed as a solution but can be taken occasionally for specifically anxiety-provoking situations. Other, non-addictive medications may be beneficial for anxiety which must be prescribed and monitored. Choosing to take medication is an individual choice, since some individuals feel that taking medication is 'giving in to' rather than fighting and preventing anxiety by looking at environmental factors and specific triggers.

- Try to identify the triggers for your anxiety. It may be hard to identify these yourself and it may beneficial to talk things through with a counsellor or psychotherapist who has a good knowledge of Asperger's syndrome. This process may help to clarify the anxiety cycle you may be experiencing.

● Find a method of relaxation which works for you as an Asperger's individual. Many traditional relaxation methods aimed at NTs may in fact be more anxiety provoking for Aspies but this is a very individual issue. Common methods include alternative/complementary therapies such as massage, hydrotherapy, herbalism, acupuncture, reflexology and so on. Deep breathing exercises are also beneficial for some.

● Meditation can work wonders; clearing the mind, inducing bodily and mental relaxation.

● Exercise, again, is very good for anxiety reduction. Any vigorous aerobic exercise (such as running, cycling, dancing) is great for using up excess energy and anxiety. Trampolining seems to be a winner, not just for kids! Yoga, pilates and similar exercises seem excellent for creating mental balance.

Social anxiety

Social anxiety could best be described as a feeling of unease and great self-consciousness when a person is in a social situation. Manifestations of social anxiety could be unusual shyness, selective mutism (speaking very little or not at all in some social situations), being unable to eat or perform an act such as writing in front of someone else, being unable to do everyday tasks such as going into shops and other public places and avoiding most social situations. Some people would argue that social anxiety is an inherent part of Asperger's syndrome. Social anxiety is also seen to co-exist or be a part of shyness. However, it is important to note that personality plays a large role in Asperger's syndrome. Some Aspies are shy by personality, others gregarious. All Aspies, whatever their personality, will experience social anxiety to a greater or lesser degree. It certainly seems a fallacy that Asperger's individuals are inherently egocentric, self-centred or disinterested in relating or empathising with others. What seems more accurate may be to suggest that it is the aspects of social interaction, social communication and flexible thinking expected by the mainstream that cause many Aspies to withdraw into themselves or avoid social contact more out of necessity than choice. If an Aspie continually experiences failures in his attempts to make social contact, be this through rejection, ridicule or bullying, it is inevitable that the individual may withdraw into himself and avoid social contact as much as possible. If you feel that you suffer from social anxiety or avoidant behaviour, seek help with this. If your mental health is suffering because of these issues, seek support.

Self-harm

Self-harm occurs when a person deliberately hurts, mutilates or injures themselves. This can be done on a regular basis or occasionally. There are multiple reasons why a person may do this. In the case of Asperger's syndrome there may also be a sensory or physiologically based component as a trigger. Commonly, individuals who self-harm may: cut, burn, pick, scratch or tear their skin; inhale or insert harmful substances or objects internally; punch, hit or throw parts of their body at things such as a wall, or pull out hair. Taking overdoses without a clear intention to commit suicide is also self-harm.

Some individuals who self-harm have clear triggers for why they self-harm such as past abuse, specific traumatic events such as loss, pressures such as social conformity, depression, low self-esteem, or emotional and social isolation. Overall, however, the trigger usually causing a person to self-harm is as an escape from psychological pain of some kind. There may be no clear trigger. In the case of autism there may be a specific sensory reason, such as wanting to experience 'real' pain.

Self-harming may be used by individuals for the following reasons: making internal pain visible on the outside as a way of communication; as a means control in an otherwise unstable world; making emotionally unbearable pain physical which may be easier to cope with; feeling 'real' or 'alive' when you feel empty or numb emotionally; as a means of releasing unbearable psychological tension or as a means of punishing the self through depression or self-hatred.

For some individuals the idea of stopping self-harming is worse than facing up to the issues which cause it. Certainly in the case of autism and Asperger's syndrome, it could be argued that taking away the coping mechanism of self-harm could be more detrimental to the individual unless a number of other complex needs are met in the individual's life. The triggers and issues surrounding self-harm in AS individuals may be very different to those of an NT so consider these issues too, such as sensory differences, physiological factors such as diet, and so on.

If you self-harm you may not be ready to stop. Seek advice from mental health services if you want professional help to stop. The key is to minimise the damaging effects of self-harm if you are not ready to stop. If you regularly badly injure yourself, ensure that you access proper medical help for injuries as they happen to minimise long-term damage.

Battling self-harm:

Firstly identify triggers when it takes place. When, where, why, who with and how? Keep a diary and monitor these details. Can you break the cycle?

When you feel you need to self-harm try to distract yourself with other activities such as talking to someone you trust; writing down your feelings in the form of a diary or letter; immersing yourself in music or a creative activity such as art; immersing yourself in the sensory environment, for example, smelling a calming scent or in exercise. These distractions are all very much easier said than done if you have already reached the stage of distress.

If you still feel you need to harm yourself try the following: use a red marker or eyeliner to mark the places you want to harm; rub ice on the parts of yourself you wish to harm; use a punchbag such as cushions, place plasters or bandages on areas you wish to harm or flick an elastic band on your wrist.

If you really cannot prevent harming yourself, ensure that you dress and care for any injuries as soon as they occur. Also, be aware that there is sometimes a lack of compassion and understanding of self-harm by the medical profession, but not seeking medical help when it is required can do more harm in the long-term.

Obsessions/rituals/compulsions/routines

In the life of an Aspie, the luxury that NT individuals take for granted is that of a relatively stable and secure existence, that is, they can, to some comfortable degree, make sense of what is going on around them. It is very much for this reason that many Aspies crave order, routine and sameness. The Aspie love of order is often seen as inflexible, resistant and unhealthy. However, if the world is so inconsistent and confusing, it is unsurprising that an AS individual will want to create order in any way that works for them. This may be engaging in activities that appear reminiscent of obsessive compulsive disorder (OCD). The key point here is to note whether removing such activities from a person might cause more distress than the acts themselves.

Counselling/therapy

Beware the terms 'counselling' and 'therapy'. There are many forms of counselling and therapy available. Some forms are better than others, the key being identifying exactly what you want to gain out of it. Some forms of counselling and therapy rely on a person looking at the root of their problems. In order to move and heal they are required to go over painful or traumatic experiences. Others can be draining in that they focus so much on the problem that an individual comes out feeling disempowered having hammered in the negativity of their situation even more. Ask yourself: are you looking to talk out your problems by being listened to, are you looking to gain self-awareness or are you seeking solutions or ways forward? Be clear about what it is you want out of the counselling or therapy before you go!

Some Aspies seek counselling as they are looking for a person with whom to navigate and make sense of an 'alien' social world. Many forms of therapy and counselling rely on introspective activity and discussion based on feelings involving emotional recognition and abstract self-awareness. This can sometimes cause more harm than good for Aspies who are not naturally wired to view the world in ways other than through logic and can end up more confused and depressed. Sadly, there aren't many practical styles of counselling or therapy readily available for Aspies at present. The ideal forms of support would capitalise and relate to the Aspie way of making sense of the world with an emphasis on practicality, structure and logic. If you are interested in seeking such support please see the contact for 'The Missing Link' at the back of the guide.

Anger towards self and others and emotional oversensitivity

As discussed in the 'Depression' section, directing anger towards yourself can have a very detrimental effect on your mental wellbeing. Living with AS can be enormously frustrating. Add that to a lack of understanding and acceptance from others and the outcome can sometimes be a lot of anger, bitterness and cynicism. However, taking anger out on yourself or others, no matter how much sense it seems to make at the time, does not help at all, often leaving regret afterwards. Anger starts in a spiral. The best way to handle it is to look for the signs before it gets out of hand. Due to the constant build up of frustration and anxiety in everyday life, becoming exhausted and overwhelmed is common for many Aspies. Aspies will have 'meltdowns' during which they may attack or lash out at others (usually in an emotional sense). The constant arousal can also lead to becoming emotionally oversensitive in situations which others would 'shrug off'. If you feel yourself starting to get stressed, angry or overloaded try the following:

- Talk to someone you trust. Sometimes talking to a person who is not directly involved with you can be more helpful as they can provide a neutral perspective.

- Escape straight away. This may mean leaving the room, going out for a walk or going for a drive.

- Have your needs understood well by NTs so that you don't have to keep explaining yourself. Have a drill whereby if overload is starting to occur others will give you their blessing to escape to your own space to 'come down' without a big emotional 'show-down'.

- Immerse yourself in something else completely such as a special interest, film, piece of music.

- Do something constructive that you normally have no motivation to do. Channel your anger into this.

- Work the anger off physically through exercise or bashing a pillow or punch bag.

- Think about someone else – could you channel your anger into helping someone else positively?

- Don't be too hard on yourself; don't strive for perfection, you are often trying your best so be proud of that.

- Don't be too hard on others, forgiveness can be helpful and empowering.

- Empower yourself with positivity and the ability to rise above what is angering you.

- Understand that you may need to support the NTs around you in removing emotion from situations where you 'meltdown'. An NT may continue to attach emotional importance to such a situation wanting to 'talk it through' and so on long after the Aspie has got over it. Try and help NTs to understand that meltdowns are more a result of over-stimulation than a major emotional issue.

Daily activity

For many AS individuals, social exclusion at some level is a reality. This may be not having a job or meaningful daily activity. This could also be through exclusion in the community, from leisure or social activities, or it could be emotional isolation from struggling to create and maintain friendships and relationships. Social exclusion therefore can often mean leaving an individual with an empty life devoid of meaning or sense. The key is to keep levels of activity up. This means keeping occupied as much as possible. An empty life allows for the most unpleasant feelings to come to the surface. Keeping the mind and body occupied reduces the chance for this to occur. In an ideal world Asperger's adults would have as much access to participation in society as everyone else. Sadly, this ideal world does not yet exist. It takes a lot of strength to keep going under these circumstances. It takes a lot of courage to carry on. If you are one of these tenacious individuals who just 'keep on going', praise yourself for doing so, and ensure that others give you credit also. This will keep your self-esteem up, where it should be.

Chapter 3

Wellbeing

Photograph by Ian Mulroy, Pilling, Lancashire

AS and wellbeing, often forgotten issues

All too frequently, AS individuals are looked at in terms of their 'disorder', 'condition' or 'problem'. The person needs to be looked at aside from the 'problem' of Asperger's syndrome before their diagnosis. Even Aspies themselves are guilty of this (perfectly understandably) in the sense that following diagnosis they can become obsessed with Asperger's syndrome and autism to the point where they can forget they are a person with a sense of individuality aside from the diagnosis. Remembering that AS is a large part of a person, it is not by any means that whole person. Looking from a holistic viewpoint as an AS individual is essential for wellbeing. It seems that rather than focusing on the 'severity' of an individual's AS and improving or changing this, it seems more useful to focus on how the individual is actually coping with it.

Special interests

Common to many Aspies is an all-encompassing interest or 'obsession'. Having an intense focus on one or two things is sometimes seen as being mentally unhealthy, causing a person to have a narrow or unrealistic understanding of the outside world. However, how many Aspies would actually want to lose their special interests or obsessions? It would undoubtedly be interesting to know. In a world that can sometimes make little sense, having an interest which does make sense to a person appears like an excellent coping and survival strategy.

Developing an Asperger's friendly culture

'If you would just try a bit harder you would find life much easier.'

'You are being deliberately inflexible and difficult.'

'You are articulate, bright and able. It's all in your head, there's nothing wrong with you.'

'If you just tried to fit in with everyone else you would be much happier.'

'You aren't on the autistic spectrum, you can talk and make eye contact!'

'Just join in with everyone else!'

'You only have to choose to be happy.'

What does it take to make others realise what it is like to have an invisible disability? Sadly, at times, creating a physical manifestation such as self-harm seems to be the only way for some individuals to get listened to. Don't be one of these. Autism and Asperger's syndrome are undoubtedly very complex conditions which are not easily understood. However, the lack of understanding and expertise among lay people and professionals alike affects those who need it the most, the AS individuals themselves. In the end, is it really worth all the mental energy it takes to fit in with others and pass off as 'normal'? Would a person paralysed from the waist down keep pushing himself to move his legs? Would a blind person keep challenging themselves to cross the road without supports? It is hard to say, since some people would argue that AS individuals are just late developers and should not be compared with individuals who have incurable disorders or impairments. Others would argue that since AS is firmly a different wiring of the brain it is simply not worth trying to alter something that isn't meant to be changed. It all seems to boil down to the diversity debate. Disclosing and acknowledging AS to others can be a truly liberating and joyful experience, and equally can backfire dramatically. Encourage an Asperger's friendly culture as much as possible. Don't accept ignorance, but don't get mad with those who don't accept it. Don't even bother. Unreasonable people cannot be reasoned with.

Personality and Asperger's syndrome

As has been mentioned throughout this guide, it is important to remember that an individual's personality has a huge impact on how they cope with their Asperger's syndrome. There is nothing worse than being faced with well-meaning individuals who try to 'support' the AS individual with stereotyped knowledge of AS, as though 'one strategy fits all Aspies'. It is certainly difficult to pick between what is the personality of an individual and what is Asperger's syndrome in an individual. This would be a long, complex and probably unfruitful exercise. However, in terms of wellbeing, truly 'being oneself' is key. Some Aspies complain that they feel as though 'they don't really exist' or have a number of personalities. One way of looking at this phenomenon might be that it is a very sensible survival strategy. If the person you know you are deep down feels to you too odd, 'off the wall' or frightful to ever be revealed it is unsurprising that you might develop a 'front' to cope. This is not the same kind of 'front' that may be exhibited by an NT. The type of 'front' or created personalities that AS individuals often have to employ to get by are much deeper and much more complex. The sheer effort of trying to behave and appear 'normal' for many

AS adults requires skill, an act which if put on for long periods can lead to exhaustion and depression, especially when it provides no particular clear gain.

Relaxation

Adequate relaxation is essential for anyone, not just people with AS. However, for individuals who suffer frequently high levels of anxiety and tension, relaxation is necessary for healthy functioning. Many Aspies live in a state of constant arousal, meaning that they have less mental energy with which to work through their own and others' emotions. Commonly, as a result, many Aspies have frequent emotional outbursts or 'meltdowns' which to NTs can seem completely out of proportion to the situation or nonsensical. For some Aspies, traditional methods of relaxation aimed at NTs do nothing for them. Is there an Aspie friendly 'sanctuary' where you can readily go to relax? This may be a place where you have total control, where your needs are met on your terms or where you can truly be free to be yourself, AS and all. No front and no acting. For many Aspies, finding a way to adequately relax may be related to a sensory need or it may be found in a special interest.

Sleep

Having AS can be exhausting. The mental energy it takes to negotiate a world not designed for Aspies is great. Combine this with sensory overload, frequent intense emotional reactions, physiological sensitivities and the fact that many individuals on the autistic spectrum seem to have unusual sleep patterns and you are looking at one tired individual! The healing benefits of good quality sleep cannot be overestimated. If you invest in anything, make it a 'haven' to sleep in. Adequate rest and sleep are essential for functioning.

Good sleeping tips for Aspies:

- Create a sanctuary which for you is conducive to good sleep. You may have sensory sensitivities you are not even aware of which may cause you to suffer from poor quality sleep. These may include distress at sleeping next to others (for no emotional reason), needing total quiet or being affected by bedclothes which are incompatible with your tactile sensory needs.

- Incorporate sleep patterns into your routine. Try and keep waking and sleeping times consistent.

- Have a waking and sleeping routine whereby you do the same things in the same order at these times. This can be very therapeutic.

- Oversleeping is just as bad as not sleeping enough. If you are prone to depression, heading for bed is often a solution. Try and find an alternative. Oversleeping can make a person more tired and weak.

- If, due to your AS, the only way you are able to sleep is at odd times for short periods or in a certain pattern, try to ensure that those around you accept that you cannot always 'fit in' with the sleep patterns of others.

Diet

Some Aspies appear very sensitive to certain foods, are 'faddy' or restricted eaters. This may have a sensory or specific physiological basis. However, aiming to eat a balanced and varied diet is something to be seriously considered. It is, without a doubt, clear that a poor diet affects mental and physical health and wellbeing. For Aspies who may be especially sensitive to certain additives and substances, eating a diet including large amounts of processed, unnatural foods seems illogical. Eating a wholly natural diet can be expensive and time-consuming. It is certainly much easier to go for the convenience option but for an Aspie the longer-term effects can be far from convenient.

Common autistic intolerances include: dairy products, yeast, gluten/wheat and artificial additives.

General things to avoid: caffeine (in tea, coffee, soft drinks), alcohol (especially if you suffer from depression/anxiety), hydrogenated fats (check labels), refined carbohydrates (in white bread, white rice), high sugar and high fat foods, artificial sweeteners (Aspartame seems to be a particular offender), artificial flavours and colours and processed foods (canned and packaged foods).

If you are not intolerant for sensory or physiological reasons try and incorporate the following into your diet:

- as many raw fruits and vegetables as possible (5 a-day)

- oily fish (sardines, mackerel, salmon)

- raw nuts and seeds

- skinless white meat (turkey and chicken)

- dried fruit

- wholegrain foods (wholemeal bread, wholemeal pasta, brown rice)

- Porridge, pulses, and beans.

General diet tips:

- Breakfast: never miss it. Incorporate breakfast always into your routine. It is essential to get your body and brain kick-started.

- Blood sugar supply: keep your blood sugar supply constant. 'Quick fix' energy foods such as chocolate or sugary foods will create a quick high but a worse low. Keeping blood sugar constant is essential for mental and physical balance. Eat a regular supply of slow-release energy foods such as nuts, fruits, grains and pulses.

- Treats: keep these as they are meant to be – treats!

- Timing of meals: try not to eat heavy foods later than 6pm at the latest as this is likely to upset adequate digestion.

Some supplements seem to have beneficial effects for some Aspies. Such supplements are linked to brain functioning. These supplements include evening primrose oil, folic acid, flaxseed oil and omega 3 fish oils.

Exercise

For some Aspies the word 'exercise' evokes memories of team sports or imposed physical activity leading to humiliation and embarrassment. The clumsiness or lack of coordination experienced by many Aspies can mean that exercising in the company of others is avoided. However, many Aspies enjoy endurance sports that are fairly solitary such as running, cycling, walking, climbing and so on. Exercise is necessary for keeping mental balance. The massive build-up of anxiety for many Aspies is often much beyond that experienced by NTs on a regular basis. Exercise is enormously helpful in reducing this anxiety. Exercise also helps the brain to release 'feel-good' chemicals which keep depression at bay. Exercise is a safe and useful way to release tension and frustrations without hurting the self and others.

Co-occuring Neurological Conditions

It is important to note that certain co-occurring neurological conditions can make a massive impact on the coping ability of an Asperger's individual. Common co-occurring conditions include dyslexia, dyspraxia, ADD, ADHD, Tourette's syndrome and others. Seek advice from professionals/supporters who have a good understanding of the impact of a number of neurological conditions occurring together and the best course of positive action.

Medication

There is currently no 'cure' for autism and Asperger's syndrome, and indeed many Aspies and Auties would ascertain that they certainly do not wish for a cure either. If they were 'cured' they wouldn't exist any more, some Aspies say. Others would choose to keep some of the positive aspects of Asperger's syndrome and dump the negative aspects. Since there is no 'cure', there is no pill or medication to be taken for AS. However, it is clear that some medications can be helpful for some of the more detrimental effects that AS and associated issues can have. The key area in which medication appears to be helpful is in reducing the negative issues associated with anxiety. Some medications are prescribed for issues which may appear a part of other disorders especially some mental illnesses. It is important to seek advice on which medications are beneficial for an individual with a different neurological make-up such as that of Asperger's syndrome.

Sensory needs

Thankfully the sensory needs of people with AS are beginning to be taken much more seriously in terms of their potential impact on functioning. Some people with AS may not actually be fully aware that their sensory style is actually very different to an NT. Having a different sensory make-up can be very disabling if not taken seriously. Sensory Integration programmes do exist, how readily is unclear. For NT individuals it can often be hard to comprehend the unusual impact of sensory input on Aspies. Don't let your needs become ignored or not respected. Assert your requirements to cope in a certain sensory environments. Don't tolerate ignorance. There are ways you can help yourself if you feel that you may have troubling responses to sensory input.

● Most important is having access to a space where you have control over your sensory environment. You may be able to create one in your home, this is your 'haven' and could be a very helpful way to gain sensory balance.

- Earplugs are extremely useful for a variety of auditory sensitivities. Also using headphones will help get through some difficult noisy environments.

- If you have food sensitivities, find out how restricted your diet may be for your health from a source such as a GP or dietician. If you have no particular goals to widen your diet, leave it!

- If being touched is an issue for you, explain to those around you that you cannot cope with light/hard touch or unexpected touch and ask them to respect your wishes not to be touched.

- If biting soothes you, obviously ask permission from others first but generally keep this urge to yourself! Good alternatives are chewing gum, chewy sweets, plastic items which are non-toxic.

- Incorporate massage into your life, Indian Head Massage is good, remedial sports massages are good for deep pressure touch. Reflexology is another option.

- 'Stress balls', blu-tack, plasticine, gel-filled products are all great for tactile balance.

- If you crave deep pressure invest in some weighty objects such as heavy blankets or by weighing yourself down with weights (not too heavy though!).

- There are a number of good vibrating massage products on the market, these can be very beneficial to reduce tactile overload or produce general sensory balance.

- If you are easily visually overloaded, keep your environment low-arousal with the level of lighting you can stand. Keep clutter to a minimum, emphasise order if that helps. Choose colours carefully. Consider tinted glasses according to your needs.

- In environments you cannot control, ask others to respect your needs. If you have a specific aversion to smells, have access to something you can carry around with you with a smell you find balancing such as on a small piece of material or in a small container.

- Be aware of fabrics when buying clothes, choose fabrics that are tolerable. You may be relaxed and tolerate them well in the shop, but would you when overloaded or stressed?

● 'White noise' can be very helpful to balance auditory overload.

Black and white thinking

One of the traps many Aspies fall into is 'black and white' or 'all or nothing' thinking. This can manifest itself in perfectionism, high anxiety levels, obsessiveness and getting 'mentally stuck'. It could be that this style of thinking is inherent to many Aspies, and rather than trying to alter it, having an awareness of the potential effects could be helpful. Indeed, this style of thinking can lead to many positive outcomes through emphasis, thoroughness, accuracy and dedication. Being systematic thinkers, some Aspies prefer there to be a logical answer to everything. One of the first, albeit difficult, things to do is to accept that often there actually are no answers or explanations to some situations, especially social situations. Frustrating as this can be, remember that although logic is helpful, it sadly cannot be applied to everything.

It is critically important to remember that the non-autistic world does not operate on this 'all or nothing' premise. The non-autistic world operates more on the grey areas in-between than the poles of black and white. This is certainly true where situations involve interpretation rather than a finite answer. This is also very true where there is an emphasis on emotional over logical responses. If you can, try and look at situations from a more balanced viewpoint, which may involve consciously thinking whether your thoughts are actually realistic, and that there may be a number of explanations. Keeping an open mind is essential. Flexible thinking is an art and takes practice.

The thinking trap

One thing many Aspies cannot be accused of is having an 'empty head' or 'vacant mind'. In order to work out the confusing NT world many Aspies have no choice but to think it all through intellectually. If you are used to doing this most days, to do the things others seem to just take for granted, it is not unlikely that at times you can't stop thinking. If you are also prone to anxiety and depression, continual thinking can be a very negative exercise. What you feed into your mind is usually how you will feel. If you feed your mind with negative and fearful thoughts, this is what your mind will believe to be true.

Some strategies for breaking the 'thinking trap'

- Keep a positive commentary going on in your mind. If anxious or depressing thoughts are beginning to take over make yourself stop the thought there and then. Ask yourself: is it helpful for me to think this way? Replace the thought with a positive or useful thought.

- Create inner peace. Remember what you feed into your brain, is what your brain will believe. Create images within your brain that make you feel good.

- Give your senses a different focus. If music helps you, lose yourself in that. If touch helps you, lose yourself in that.

- Keep telling yourself that you are in control of your mind. Giving yourself positive talk will provide positive feelings.

Cumulative positive experiences

For an Asperger's individual whose experience includes a number of negative experiences, it is unsurprising that as a survival strategy they may begin to avoid many situations which involve a form of social contact. However, this survival strategy can backfire in the long-term. Many Asperger's individuals exhibit great strength in that they refuse to give up. If you don't try, you will never know. If you are tempted to avoid a situation, ask yourself, 'Might it be different this time?' (if you have been there before). If it is a new situation, accept that fear of the unknown and of change is hard for many Asperger's individuals. Give yourself credit for the changes you have made, even if they are only small ones. Use the success you have had to spur you on to make more gradual changes. Try and face your fears of the unknown to try new experiences, since the experience may be something beneficial and if you didn't try it you would never know.

Some Asperger's individuals struggle with beginning and ending tasks that do not make full sense to them or that they are not particularly interested in. This can lead to lack of motivation and difficulties with concentration and staying on task. Having others around to keep an individual on task through encouragement and prompts is very helpful in gaining a 'portfolio' of positive experiences to build on.

Whatever you do, don't constantly compare yourself with others, including other Aspies and especially neurologically typical individuals. This could lead you into nothing but negativity, envy, anger or bitterness.

Natural approaches

The power of nature cannot be underestimated as a therapeutic medium. Some Aspies appear to be especially sensitive to some substances including certain additives, chemicals, atmospheric changes, environmental changes and so on. Choosing a natural approach to finding an Aspie-friendly balance in a variety of areas in life is worth a go. Living in harmony with nature's rhythms and gifts is not easy in a heavily developed world. Nature can be very helpful in restoring sensory, behavioural and emotional balance. Some popular natural approaches include:

Herbalism: The use of herbs and plants as alternative remedies.

Aromatherapy: Using oils derived from plant essences through inhalation, massage or in bathing.

Massage: The different sensory profile experienced by many Aspies in terms of tactile stimulation can be greatly benefitted through massage.

Reflexology: Manipulation of the feet in order to break down energy-blocking deposits in areas of the body.

Flower essences: Essences of particular flowers can be used to combat negative emotions.

Hydrotherapy: Using water and steam as a therapeutic medium in the form of massage, inhalation, taking internally, swimming, bathing.

Equine and animal therapeutic input

For many people, not just some Aspies, contact with animals can be enormously therapeutic. Animals as therapy and as practical helpers (in the case of physical or sensory disabilities) are common in the UK. However, there are fewer such 'service animals' (mainly dogs) readily available for people with autism in the UK. An animal companion or simply spending time with animals (if a person likes them), is so beneficial. Social interaction can be greatly helped by the presence of animals. For a start animals always provide a talking point, making small-talk easier. Also, if a person is struggling with a conversation or is having anxiety in a social situation, an animal can provide a welcome distraction from the person with AS. Having access to an animal is an excellent antidote to loneliness. Animals are certainly not a substitute for human interaction, but the physical closeness by stroking an animal can provide affection and sensory balance. Animals can also provide practice in building interactional skills for people who otherwise would struggle to interact with anything other than their computer or inanimate objects.

In the case of horses, Equine Assisted Psychotherapy (EAP), used currently with mental health problems, also has potential benefits for individuals on the autistic spectrum.

Life with Asperger's syndrome and horses

By Miss G Edmonds, 2004

For as long as I can remember I have always felt a natural empathy with non-human species – not aliens I hasten to add! This empathy is with the animal species equus, i.e. the horse. When I look back through photos spanning the 25 years of my life I can find many photos of me with horses and other animals appearing to be in natural harmony. I am never happier then when hacking out in the countryside, cantering across a field or just being around horses. In fact, a lot of the time I wonder if I actually relate better to horses than to people! The language of the horse is something I seem to innately understand. It is a complex language, which relies on visual associations. It can be learnt through theory and tapping deliberately into the psychology of the horse. Some years ago I began to consolidate what I felt I innately experienced around horses by reading material on the psychology of horses. It dawned on me that it already was quite natural to me, and that a lot of it I found I subconsciously already understood.

Around this time last year, I was diagnosed with Asperger's syndrome. This did not come as a shock to me as I had suspected as much for about a year and years earlier had suspected that there was something different about me. However, I had no name for what it was or even any idea that I could be on the autistic spectrum. This was something I had only ever associated with the people I had got to know on voluntary befriending schemes and social groups that I helped out with at organisations such as Mencap and Barnardos. These individuals had severe learning difficulties and didn't relate, or who related in very challenging ways, to other people. Little did I imagine that I could have more in common with my autistic cousins than with neurotypicals! Although, I must admit that I always enjoyed the company of these challenging individuals but never knew why until now!

I also began to reflect recently as to why I also always felt so happy in the company of animals, most notably with horses. Whilst engaging in research on autism and Asperger's syndrome I stumbled across the work of Temple

Grandin, and realised that I knew exactly where she was coming from. I would dearly love to meet Temple someday as I fully agree with and respect her theories and views on the humane and successful handling of certain animals by viewing things from their point of view. In her article, *Thinking The Way Animals Do*, Temple explains a number of points which identify the links between the behaviour and outlook of horses and autistic individuals.

I have learnt through my own observation and experiences, now that I am aware of my own autism, that those who handle horses and other animals in a wholly neurotypical way tend to achieve less of a bond and fewer trusting relationships with them. I spend a lot of time around them both talking to them, caring for them and of course, horse-riding! They belong to Vicky Bliss, a psychologist who specialises in learning disabilities and the autistic spectrum. Vicky shares my approach to the horses, an approach often called natural horsemanship, which considers the good of the horse over human desires. This approach is championed by famous horse personalities such as US-based Monty Roberts and UK-based Kelly Marks.

In his book, *Horse Sense for People*, Monty Roberts describes his observations of traits autistic individuals and horses have in common. Such things are:

● Fear of loud and unusual sounds.

● Thriving on routine.

● Distress at direct eye contact.

● Dislike of forced touch.

● Distress at unfamiliar sights and sounds.

Monty Roberts describes his belief that perhaps it is not surprising that the horse, a visual thinker with an extraordinary ability to sense the intentions of its rider, is quite comfortable being ridden by autistics and, furthermore, is able to cope with their often unusual behaviour. (Taken from *Horse Sense For People*: 2000: p. 45.)

Hence, from my own experiences I can now understand and feel very glad that my Asperger's syndrome has significantly enhanced my relationships with animals, especially horses. This example of unusual skill is one of many factors that support my view that the unique psyche of the individual with autism has an enormous contribution to make to our world. I believe that the autistic way of thinking, which is often highly creative, unusual and alternative can only serve to enrich the lives of others when allowed to blossom in the appropriate environment.

Taken from The National Autistic Society Website www.autism.org.uk

Chapter 4

Positive attributes of Asperger's syndrome

In this chapter we will individually examine what we perceive as being the most relevant positive attributes of Asperger's syndrome and look at how these might translate into society.

Please note:

The characteristics chosen are not 'given' traits of AS individuals, hence the term 'individual'. Personality, as we have discussed, plays a very large role in determining the presentation of an AS adult. The characteristics outlined here are generally discussed as being common in people with AS, however that does not mean to say that they are exhibited by each and every Aspie in any way shape or form!

Making the most of yourself

Among certain groups a model with an emphasis on the deficits and disorders associated with Asperger's syndrome seems to dominate. This may be helpful in certain instances in the AS person's life such as seeking diagnosis (if this is helpful, which it usually is) and medical intervention. However, such emphasis on this medical model approach appears to be less helpful when ensuring that Asperger's individuals have a quality of life and adequate participation in society. It is essential not only to emphasise the positive and useful aspects of Asperger's syndrome but also to look at these aspects in reality (not isolation). What follows are the traits of Asperger's syndrome we believe an individual could strive to make the most of.

Routines

In some cases following routines can restrict some important activities. However, there are some positives to following routines because it means that you have a system in place and things get done. In some jobs it can be very useful because the employer can rely on you if you do the same tasks in the same order each time, and they would know that you would cover everything that needed to be done. The advantages in everyday life of following routines are vast, provided that those around are able to accept a less spontaneous and chaotic style of life. Thankfully there are NTs who have the cognitive flexibility to see the advantages of structure and routine, but some individuals are less insightful.

Dislike of trends

Aspies often think logically and one aspect of logical thinking is not following trends. We all have to wear clothes to stay warm and indeed if we did not wear clothes while outside we would be arrested. It is not unusual for someone on the autistic spectrum to simply wear clothes purely because they would feel cold if they did not, and therefore they will simply buy something that will stop them from feeling cold. Such Aspies would therefore deviate from following the latest trend and would not deliberately buy clothes with designer labels.

This can be very positive behaviour because the Aspie is not being swayed by 'group mentality' which tends to be based on a group of people following the leader, but not really appearing to make decisions for themselves, independently of how their peers think. Most Aspies have a much greater sense of individuality and wears whatever they want to wear, and does not allow end up spending a large proportion of their money on fashions and unnecessary possessions simply to try and be accepted. Such individuals may not care if people do not like the clothes they wear or the possessions they have. They can't quite understand why people would think that there is anything wrong with just wearing clothes that you feel comfortable in, as long as they are in a reasonable condition, or possessing objects to be thrown away as the next trend arrives. For some the 'comfort' factor is of overriding importance and clothes have to be free of labels and washed many times to soften them before they are fit to wear. These considerations are experienced as much more important than 'fashion'.

It is undoubtedly positive to think that way about clothing, because substance is certainly far more important than appearance, unless of course you are attending a formal occasion where smart attire is expected, such as a job interview. However, there could be scenarios where a group rejects you due to the way you dress or you have difficulty attracting a partner. Don't let it bother you, because each and every person who is judging you on what you wear truly is shallow-minded, and it is not ideal to have shallow-minded friends. If you do try to emulate other people too much, you are more likely to attract those kinds of people. However, you may have your own style and take a carefree approach, deciding that people can take you as you are or not at all. Even if it should turn out that the majority of people take you not at all, the advantage of this is that the people who do take you as you are are likely to be more genuine and to make better friends.

Apart from the fact that you may choose not to wear what the majority are wearing, you may actually be creating your own unique style of dress sense, and this may even be inspiring to other people. There are certainly more free-thinking individuals who buy only clothes that interest them, and some may even make their own or find some bargains in market stalls. These might look more interesting than the clothes the crowd is wearing and some people may even compliment you on this. This also saves having to worry about wearing clothes which are described as 'so last season'.

Unique problem-solving

Problem-solving comes into everyday life and covers just about everything we ever do. The word 'problem' does not mean that something is wrong. Even crossing an empty road is solving a problem. The only difference is that as children we had to be watched and told to look both ways. As adults we may instinctively know what to do without thinking about it. Without knowing, we are still solving a problem, just as working out a sum in your head is solving a problem even if it does only take you a split second to work out.

We tend to only call something a problem whenever it does not go entirely according to plan and from time to time things do happen that take more effort to resolve, because the people involved in the situation have perhaps not had this situation occur before. If you are in such a situation at present, you might think of a solution that no one else does. As an Aspie, you might happen to have a knack for thinking of something creative which actually works. If you have low self-esteem then every time you come up with a solution to a problem that people seem to appreciate then feel proud of yourself. If your different way of looking at the problem was related to your unique thinking style as an Aspie, then this is something to look at as a positive point of being a person with Asperger's syndrome. Your unique problem-solving abilities might one day even help to save someone's life.

Every time we have learnt something new, we have solved a problem. Although we may know automatically how to do these things without thinking, we have not always known. A problem does not automatically mean that the person who has to solve the problem is unlucky. That does not mean that the hungry person is unlucky, as hunger is natural and they will find some food and satisfy their hunger.

Problem-solving is something which Aspies often enjoy. The problem which they are trying to solve may not necessarily be a case of something being wrong. For example, the Aspie might be working in a training organisation and be asked to produce a timetable for when next year's classes will take place. This does not mean that the Aspie is resolving something that went wrong, but the actual problem that is being solved is matching classes up to tutors within certain time constraints without anyone being timetabled in two places at one time. It may sound like a very simple task, but in practice it is much more challenging. Most people attempting such a task would constantly find clashes taking place or other unsatisfactory results such as a class having two teachers for the same subject or the same subject twice on the same day. Therefore a technique needs to be developed to minimize these problems as much as the restraints of the timetable would allow.

This can be positive because solving a complicated problem can give the individual a real sense of achievement, and also helps the individual to keep his mind active. This is good because it can prevent the onset of unwanted negative feelings such as boredom or loneliness. Not keeping the mind active can be very unhealthy and potentially lead to mental health problems, which is why it is positive to spend time solving problems. Some great innovations can be solved in this way, simply by the innovator sitting at home drawing something on a piece of paper and thinking, 'What if?' While their peers are at the pub or somewhere else with their friends, the individual in her bedroom can come up with a innovative ideas. Maybe many years later her idea will come to life in people's homes all around the country or perhaps the world. People with Asperger's syndrome or other autistic spectrum disorders can contribute respected ideas and solutions, valued by society.

It may be that most NT's have abilities in several areas that you feel that you are weak in but that there is one thing that you are able to do exceptionally well. If this is the case, then now is the time to stop feeling unhappy about all the things that you find hard and to get a buzz out of the thing that you can do exceptionally well or have a specialist knowledge about. Even if there has been little call in your life for your knowledge, perhaps because the topic matter is slightly unusual, there will probably be a use for it somewhere even if this involves moving to a different part of the country or possibly even a different country altogether. Or it may mean that such opportunities are rare and patience may be necessary. It could take years, but may be well worth waiting for.

Memory

Having a good long-term memory is obviously very positive because it will help you to recall past events that other people may have forgotten about entirely. Of course this will help you to be able to reminisce about fond memories from the past, as other people who shared the experience with you may have no recollection. It is equally positive having a good memory for facts and figures. It is very useful because the majority of individuals tend not to remember small details quite as much. In contrast many Aspies often know a very minor fact such as someone's middle name, a reference number or the date when something took place a few years ago. In everyday life, the advantage can be that you are like a 'walking encyclopedia'. At home, for instance, you might be asked the date of a relative's birthday and also remember their age, which is handy if it is a big birthday such as eighteen or sixty. Another everyday situation in which it could be an advantage is if someone stops to ask you for directions, and you are able to explain in graphic detail how to get to the destination that they are looking for. Sadly such gifts often attract ridicule or bullying behaviour. The reason for this is not clear, and at times keeping such talents under wraps is a necessity – but do not lose sight of these gifts, since among the right people and in the right environment they may be very much appreciated.

Lively interest in a single topic

People with AS often have a very lively interest in one specific topic. Sometimes, this might be so intense that it could be classed as an obsession. Sometimes this can be unhealthy and people may have been told to stop boring everyone by talking incessantly about their chosen subject. However, there can always be positives about having such a lively interest in a narrowly chosen subject. While you are still studying you may be able to do a project on your topic, which may boost your overall grades. There might even be a university course in your chosen topic. You may think that your interest is too random, but some very obscure subjects have been studied to degree level, so it might be worth seeing whether your interest is one of them. Even if there is no course in your chosen subject, there may still be a module on it in a particular degree, and perhaps you can develop this into a career.

You can use your interest for good, maybe make a career of it or start up a club for your interest, unless one already exists. If your chosen topic is so unusual that you can not find other people in your area with a similar interest, you could type in the name of your interest on any good search engine on the Internet. Look for a message board where you can meet other people with the same interest. If one does not exist, you could quite easily set up your own basic website at no cost. If it is a very unusual type of interest it might emerge that some of the other people whom you meet through this interest are also on the Autistic spectrum.

If your interest is something which can be pursued anywhere in the world, it may be that pursuing it on a holiday could make it much more fascinating for you. Or it may make your life fascinating wherever you go and indeed you could become an expert in your chosen area of interest which may be very useful to the general public or perhaps even to important people or organisations.

Some special interests might be considered rather unusual by many people. For instance, a person with AS may be fascinated by the dimensions of cathedrals. Although following a single hobby intensely can be problematic in some ways, it can be positive in other ways. It is certainly better to be focused on the same thing all the time than to have no interests whatsoever. The hobby can be a good 'friend' because it gives the individual with AS something to think about, and can largely prevent or at least reduce negative thoughts that the person might otherwise feel. Having an intense interest in a hobby can be useful in some job situations. For instance, if you have an interest in televisions, you could do very well working in a shop which sells televisions. An interest in trains could make you a model employee on the railways. This could also have advantages in everyday life as people may come to you to ask questions based on your hobby if they are thinking of making a related purchase. If social interaction is difficult for you, the interest can be a great way of creating safe social relationships. Even if these are fairly superficial, they are still more rewarding than none at all. For example, if you know everything there is to know about cars, then your relatives might take you along to car showrooms if they are wishing to buy one so that you can advise them on whether the salesperson is giving them reliable information or not.

Talents

There are some gifted Aspies. For instance, you might be outstanding at playing music and be able to learn it with ease, or have a special talent for a particular type of drawing. Even Aspies who are not necessarily gifted might still have special talents. Talents are not always clear-cut since they are often equated with stereotypical gifts. As mentioned elsewhere in this book, some Aspies are exceptional at an academic subject such as maths or science. Someone else might have a special talent for drama, making a particular type of item or memorising the layout of a town just by reading the map of it before visiting. If you do not have a talent, are you certain of that fact? How do you know that you do not have a talent if you have not attempted everything? Maybe you are good at some sort of sport, or perhaps you are a born entertainer and do not even know how funny you are and how much pleasure and joy you've given to people. You may even have cheered someone up. You might, in particular, be appreciated by older people.

Intelligence

Asperger's individuals often have average or above-average intelligence. It does happen that Asperger's individuals obtain the highest possible grades in many subjects upon leaving school, and those who do not achieve this are usually no less intelligent than those who do, and should not underestimate their capabilities if their grades are average. Some people with Asperger's syndrome are able to go to university – receiving disappointing grades at school does not mean that this can never happen. It does not matter that this may mean starting university a year or so later, as many people do. It is rare for everyone starting a degree course to all be the same age. Most courses have some students over twenty-five. It is not at all unusual even for people in their forties or older to study for degrees. This means that if you are over forty and never went to university you still might be able to, and it is possible that experience of life is a good enough qualification to go on a degree course.

For Aspies who struggled through school as their learning style did not fit with the majority, it is possible to catch up in an AS friendly way. It is not essential to take the standard qualifications that most other people take. There are usually vocational courses which may be taken as an alternative way of obtaining a place at university. For many people, standard qualifications are not easy to get a pass mark in and this may be even more difficult for someone who has difficulty studying by traditional methods. Vocational courses are often very coursework orientated and can usually be passed by anyone who obtained a place on the course, provided that they make an appropriate effort. The only exception to the rule tends to be if the wrong course has been chosen, so thought should be given to ensuring it should be the right course. Vocational courses often provide a reasonably easy route into some universities but may need average marks rather than a bare pass. Chances will be enhanced if a high grade is achieved in some modules. If you are contemplating further study, remember, do not underestimate your capabilities. Provided that you choose a suitable course, you may surprise yourself at how well you are able to do. you may have had some negative experiences and so have a low opinion of yourself. However, you have many special capabilities and you are able to achieve as much if not more than the average person.

It would be easy to think of university courses as daunting, especially at degree level. As on a vocational course, if you have chosen the right subject you may be able to pass most, if not all, of your coursework, receiving average or above-average marks. If you have difficulty with examinations, your coursework mark should usually make up for examination marks falling below the pass mark. If, in your first year, most of your marks are not above average, do not despair as you may make progress later on in the course. Where in your first year, you may have averaged a low grade, in the final year you will probably obtain an average or above-average grade and may well pass each piece of work that you hand in. Having said this, do not be complacent, as people with AS sometimes need to try that little bit harder!

Once you have obtained a degree, you may have opportunities of further study available to you. If you eventually follow a Doctorate course, as a person with Asperger's syndrome with a unique thinking style, you might have no difficulty coming up with a thesis that has never been thought of by anyone else before! With your unique perceptions you could produce a first class thesis.

The advantages of having a degree are that it can open up more job opportunities to you and provide a great sense of achievement. No matter what other difficulties you may have encountered in your life, no one can take away this achievement and it cannot be belittled. No matter where you took your degree or what classification you obtained, your degree is still something to be proud of.

Ability at language

Ability at language is also not uncommon among people with Asperger's syndrome. Some Aspies have superb spelling and a pedantic eye for correct grammar. There are several careers in which this could be a godsend. This means that Aspies could make good writers and therefore be good at writing business reports etc. This is very positive and it is useful because any correspondence you send may impress. For instance, if you send an application form for a job with no spelling mistakes and good grammar, you have an advantage over everyone else, because it is surprising how many people make frequent spelling or grammatical errors. The advantages in everyday life are that it is easier to make yourself understood in a number of complicated situations, for example, when you need help or are helping others.

Through this aptitude some Aspies will develop a passion for foreign languages, which is indeed a very positive thing as it is a special talent if you can speak more than one language fluently. Naturally, this is very useful if you are ever visiting the country where that language is spoken with people who have no knowledge of the language – you will be indispensable. The advantages in everyday life are that you will be able to understand if a speaker of that language happens to approach you in the street and it will solve any difficulties if the person does speak your language but not fluently.

In the workplace, a good grasp of the English language or foreign languages could be very useful. In your everyday life, having a high level of accuracy in English will mean that you are better able to communicate with organisations with which you are having problems. You may be able to better understand any complex style of writing adopted by the organisation and to write back to them clearly or convey your message well over the telephone. People with AS are often very anxious at the prospect of using the telephone for such matters, however they are often better at dealing with the situation itself when they feel the fear and do it anyway. Perseverance certainly pays off because even if on the first occasion you felt that your worst fears were realised, this may simply have been because you allowed nerves to get the better of you.

Certainly in a job interview you could stand out from the crowd if you are the only applicant with fluency in a foreign language.

A love of learning

Asperger's individuals often adore learning, especially factual learning. This does not necessarily refer to going to educational establishments and sitting behind a desk. We start learning before we are even born, and the saying 'you learn something new every day' is very true. Perhaps this willingness to absorb new facts is one of the reasons why people with AS so often have above-average intelligence and are in some cases gifted? A love of learning is useful because there will be situations in which you need to learn something very quickly, and other people might not be interested enough to learn. This could make you a model employee in a number of jobs. The advantages in everyday life are that you could solve household problems quite quickly. For instance, if you are technically minded, you might be able to learn how to use a piece of new household equipment that no one else understands. One area in which Aspies are renowned for being quick learners is with computers, as even for applications that they have not previously used they can often pick up the basics with relative ease. This can be relevant to Aspies of all ages because no one is ever too old to learn.

Study is not just about going to school, college or university five days a week, as many adults of all ages attend one class a week maybe in the evening. This does not have to be for a formal qualification. Many study out of pure interest or just for fun. It is a good way to keep your mind active and will also give you the opportunity to meet other people with an interest in the same subject. Studying can help mental health and self-esteem in a short frame of time.

Attention to detail

Aspies are notorious for having a good eye for detail, and this can only be a good thing. Of course, there are cases where paying attention to the smaller details can get in the way of seeing the bigger picture. Sometimes spotting the smaller details is very useful, and such ability could make you an indispensable employee, as you will often notice things that other people did not. For instance you might ask why something is the way it is, and your manager might say they were totally unaware and thank you for bringing it to their attention. Sometimes this attention to detail can involve dates and numbers. Some Aspies, as young children, would stun their parents and others who knew them because they could work out quickly in their head what day of the week an occasion would fall on several months in advance.

Attention to detail could be useful in everyday life because you might notice something while out and about that needs attention as soon as possible. For instance, you might spot a potential safety hazard that no one else has and report it to the relevant authorities and prevent an accident or even save lives. Another example where attention to detail might come in handy is if you know the date of birth of everyone you are related to or work with, and therefore someone at work might be given a surprise fortieth birthday party that they will always cherish, which would never have taken place if you hadn't one day piped up and said, 'Do you know that John will be forty next Friday?'

Some people with AS very much like to be meticulously organised. There are some AS people who do have difficulty with this in some ways but not others. Having the ability to be organised, or even just the intention, is a really positive quality, because there are so many people who do not even care about organisation and just leave things to fester. For instance, if you were ever a student sharing a house with others, you probably noticed how little regard your housemates had for washing the dishes or keeping the house tidy in general! Perhaps you were always clearing away after them, or maybe you were the one who always seemed to have to pay the utility companies, because no one else seemed in the slightest bit concerned about this. If this is you then it is very positive that you have such a strong sense of responsibility. For those that have difficulty being organised there are ways to combat this. Carrying a 'to do list' around with you would be a good starting point, and having a notice board where you are likely to see it and you can pin reminders onto it.

Being organised in this way is of course very useful as your plans run more smoothly. Even if the most organised you ever manage to be is to put your entire collection of maps into alphabetical order, this is still useful. It means that if a relative comes round who is going abroad, you can quickly locate all the maps you have for the country they are visiting. The advantages in everyday life are that things will operate far more smoothly and it avoids the confusion of not knowing where something is when you need it.

Perseverance and dedication

Perseverance is a key word in the world of Asperger's syndrome. Of course, it can be easy to give up if things simply do not appear to be going in your favour. However, some people with AS keep trying at something no matter how many times they don't get it right and this can only be positive. For example, consider the number of people who only pass their driving test on the fifth or sixth attempt. Imagine if they had given up after their third or fourth attempt? If you can master learning how to drive then you can master just about anything through perseverance, so it certainly comes in handy to believe in the phrase, 'If at first you don't succeed, try, try again.'

A positive aspect of this way of thinking may be that you finish everything that you start and take care of every detail which you consider to be important.

Being dedicated means that you do not drop out of something even if three-quarters of the other people in the same situation do. For instance, you might be the sort of person who would follow through fully with a college or university course, even if you find it hard to fit in with the other students. If you were in a situation where the last person to give in wins some sort of prize, then part of your Asperger's syndrome may make you so dedicated that you would be the prize winner with no problems.

In the workplace, dedication is a fantastic quality. Dedication in the workplace could be seen as a marvellous gift to an employer, as it may actually be quite rare. You might be so dedicated to the organisation that you work for that you might eventually be by far the longest serving employee. You could then be a great asset to the organisation. Even if you are not a great people person, your inside-out knowledge may put you in a very strong position and give you confidence in your abilities.

Dedication to your family and friends is certainly a great quality because that way you will never lose touch with your parents when you leave home, and might also keep in regular contact with siblings, which without your dedicated attitude may well not happen. This would be even nicer for you when your own children move away from home, because it would be a shame to lose touch with them.

Dedication to a hobby or leisure activity can also be positive if you are using your brain and being creative. If you become good at the activity this can be a great boost to your self-esteem and you may be better at the activity than anyone else you know. It may even create an aspect of the activity that did not exist before or create a brand new leisure pursuit! Dedication to a physical activity is very positive because this can keep you very fit and healthy, although you should not overdo it.

Reliability

A good quality of having AS could be that in certain situations, you are very reliable. Many Asperger's individuals do what they say they are going to do and generally expect others to do the same. This is a very good quality to have as there are so many unreliable people in the world. We have all had to work in a group and felt frustrated because someone in that group doesn't do what they say they're going to do, or does it at the very last minute. Though it is not always the case, it is not uncommon for Aspies to do exactly what they say they are going to do.

Sometimes people will even be surprised because people do not usually do what they say they are going to do to the precise detail, but people with AS often have a very good eye for detail which can mean that they do not miss out anything. In fact, they can become very frustrated if they are unable, for whatever reason, to do something that they were meaning to do, even if 99% of what they had planned to do was covered. They might not like the fact that they feel stress so easily over something that really does not matter such a great deal, but the positive side of this is that people will appreciate the thoroughness which derives from this.

In a project, you could be a good project partner. Even if you sit listening for most of the time and not adding your own piece, what little you do say is probably very valuable. You may be an asset to the group because even if you do not contribute a great quantity of ideas, the ideas you do contribute are of a great quality. Better still, you may always turn up to every meeting, listen to everything that is said and when you say you are going to do something, you do exactly what you say you are going to do and when you say you are going to do it. For instance, the group leader tells the rest of the group that they need to have the next part of the project ready on Friday. The other two members of the group do not have their part of the project ready, but you do. So, even if you do not always say much and perhaps feel that you do not contribute very much, you are possibly the most reliable member of the group and those who care about the project will appreciate this. Not only do you produce the work on time with no short cuts, but the quality of the work is often very good and possibly even unique and creative.

Good timekeeping and attendance

Throughout your entire life, being on time for everything will be a widely respected quality. Many Aspies are very punctual. Punctuality is a very positive quality in the workplace because employees who are regularly late are putting their jobs at risk, and also running the risk that their employer will be reluctant to provide them with a reference if they move on to a different organisation.

In everyday life, the advantages of being on time are that people are not left waiting for you, as people who arrive for things on time would not expect to have to wait too long for the person they are meeting. This is especially important when new groups are forming or new members are joining. Latecomers can disrupt the process of the meeting. It will certainly help to be on time if you are meeting a potential partner, as this could impress them.

As well as always being on time for things, Aspies are often good at doing the number of hours that they are required to put in. For example, if they work flexi-time, they will usually work the correct hours and never falsify. People may believe that no one says anything if they add a few minutes on here and there. However, management are probably aware of this whether they let on or not, so they will be impressed by any employees that they know actually correctly enter their hours and are more likely to give them a promotion. Indeed, punctual employees have better promotion prospects than those who are more carefree about when they turn up for work or meetings.

Along the same lines as timekeeping is attendance itself. Regular attendance at college, university or work is a very positive thing. At work, this can certainly improve promotion prospects and more work will be produced by the employee, who will also seem more loyal and dedicated to their job and to the organisation.

Good timekeeping and attendance would be very good if you were to start your own business, as you would have more dedication and take the running of your business seriously. Many people, being self-employed, would sleep in and decide that they do not need to go in at 9 o' clock if they do not want to. This is true, but it is not the best way to run a business unless it is a very small sideline, which could run alongside a standard full-time job. This is because the business owner could fall behind on their work and customers might be waiting too long and becoming impatient. Aspies are often so meticulous that even when they are running their own business they would have the discipline to work all the hours and this would give them an extra chance of their business being a success.

Also, sticking to an intended time for doing things can have advantages, such as not turning up somewhere you were planning to go when it's closed.

Following rules

It is a very positive thing if you follow rules and the law. Many people do not believe in doing everything 'by the book' and believe in the saying 'rules are there to be broken'. They do not respect the rules, and will always be bound by what they want to do and not necessarily by what is and what is not legal. Perhaps, when you were younger, other people tried to persuade you to do something that you felt was wrong and maybe you were ostracised if you refused to do it. Maybe you were actually bullied into something that you knew was wrong and now feel ashamed that you did it. The important thing is that, whether you actually did something wrong or not, that if it is against your character to do something illegal or wrong, then throughout your life you will rarely break any rules or laws.

People who break laws often get found out even if it is years later, so it is better to abstain from law-breaking activities than to take part. Therefore, if you have not been on the wrong side of the law, then you should be pleased that you haven't thrown away your future with such a discrepancy. If having Asperger's syndrome is the reason that you have been so rule-bound and stayed out of trouble then that is a positive thing.

Some Aspies are such sticklers for following the rules that they would even worry about leaving a building through the entrance when its says 'Fire Exit'. People with AS can be so law-abiding that even when they have not broken any rules they can feel almost guilty. For example, a security guard might keep looking at them, so they feel nervous even though they have not stolen anything. This means that the Aspie in question is a very honest-minded person and that is a very positive attribute.

Having a keen sense of following the rules would also be beneficial if you were to start up your own business. There would be an increased possibility that you would be allowed to do so and furthermore you are less likely, as a law-abiding citizen, to break any laws in order to make more profits or to unduly influence a potential business partner. Not all self-employed people are honest so if you ever run your own business you can pride yourself on the fact that you are honest.

A romantic partner may like someone who follows rules as they will have more respect for them, and feel better able to trust and rely on them. Therefore, although people with AS can find it more difficult to find a partner, AS males especially, when they do, they often make a very good partner. Younger Aspies may invariably be rejected by potential partners because younger people are looking for fun, and may at that age actually prefer someone who breaks the rules. Another factor may be that young people would often not want to date someone who their parents would approve of, because then he or she 'must be too boring and sensible'. However, as people mature they grow tired of the 'bad boys' and 'bad girls' because they are often let down by them, and prefer someone more dependable. People with Asperger's syndrome often score very highly in this department, so if you are a young Aspie and still single then this may be because you are mature beyond your years in some ways. For the exact same reason you will have a better chance of finding a partner when you are closer to thirty. That does not mean that you definitely won't meet someone until then. If you do have to wait until then the person will be worth waiting for, and you may have a greater chance of a stable relationship in some ways, due to some of the positive attributes of your AS.

Keeping confidences

At work, you may find things out which you are not allowed to discuss anywhere else, and possibly not even among other employees. It is a good quality to be able to refrain yourself from telling anyone else what you found out. Some official information at work is classed as 'Private and Confidential'. If you are able to not mention such information, this is very positive because you will be able to keep your job, as sharing confidential information is likely to result in disciplinary action and could potentially lead to eventual dismissal from your organisation.

In the family, the ability to keep confidences could be a good quality. For instance, a sibling might want to be able to confide in you about something which they feel unable to tell your parents about. It is great if you are always willing to listen to their problem without them fearing that you will mention it to your parents. If they felt unable to trust you to keep a confidence they would possibly just keep the problem to themselves and it may grow worse.

If you are good at keeping confidences, you could find yourself in a similar situation in a friendship to that with a sibling. It is positive because this friend might consider you to be such a good listener and so non-judgmental that you become very close friends. You might even be able to attract friends as a result of your ability to keep confidences.

Bluntness and candour

A characteristic of Asperger's syndrome could be that the individual is very blunt or candid in what they say. Of course, this can sometimes cause offence and is not always appropriate. However, there are cases where being blunt and upfront can have its advantages. For instance, although it is generally not polite to tell someone they are overweight, by doing so you may be inadvertently making someone with a severe weight problem start thinking about their weight problem and they might lose weight and start to live a healthier lifestyle. We are not suggesting that you adopt the habit of making personal remarks towards strangers! However, having a blunt tongue could mean that amongst family and friends you don't 'beat about the bush', you simply tell them what you are thinking and this avoids the need for the social lies which are the norm in the NT world and not always constructive. For example, a woman goes out and buys a new dress. She wears it to a party and asks several people what they think of it. They all hate the dress and feel embarrassed to be seen with her while she is wearing it, but everyone is too polite to tell her so say that the dress is nice and that it suits her. She then asks her daughter with Asperger's syndrome what she thinks of the dress. The daughter, without emotion, tells her mother, 'I think it looks disgusting.' Everyone looks on with dropped jaws expecting some kind of commotion, but the next thing they witness is the woman giving her daughter a hug and saying 'Thank you. At least one person is honest enough to tell me the truth'. We would suggest caution where candour is used and advise that you don't single an individual out because you dislike them or find them strange.

Strong sense of social justice and compassion

Although Aspies are seen to struggle with empathy (thinking in another person's shoes) they are seen to excel in compassion (sympathising with others in a similar situation). Used to being the underdog, many Aspies strive towards social justice sometimes with fierce passion. This can lead to some Aspies being enormously caring and devoted individuals. The effects of long-term exclusion, having one's better nature being taken advantage of, bullying or teasing, plus having a strong long-term memory can lead to grudges that never end, or can lead to fiercely fighting injustice. If this is you, it may be an idea to use your grudges towards a useful purpose – channel that anger into fighting for the underdog.

For example, you may know a person who treats people badly but other people just put up with it. You may have a life-long grudge against a person for something that they did about twenty years ago but don't even remember doing themselves. You might remind them of this and it may help them to think about how they treat people. They would probably feel very upset to think that something they did so long ago has had such a profound negative impact on someone and this might force them to alter their behaviour and make them a better person.

Many Aspies are brave enough to stand up for what they believe in. Some Aspies are by nature very quiet and introverted people and could sit in a meeting not saying much until an issue comes up that they feel very strongly about and this is when they become very vocal and will do whatever they feel needs doing to fight for their issue. Action might include persuading people to sign a petition, standing on the street alone with a placard and shouting out what they want to see happen, lobbying political headquarters or even organising a march. These are more extreme examples and we certainly don't advise causing a public nuisance or breaking the law. Sometimes taking the angry approach is not constructive because it can seem too emotionally charged, but if you are able to gather evidence from other people about an issue that you're passionate about then maybe you're the ideal person to take action in a logical and constructive way and make people listen. Your actions might even change a particular aspect of life for dozens, thousands or (who knows) millions of people for the better and you might become a public hero or heroine.

Ability to dissociate logic from emotion

Frequently, Aspies have been viewed as robotic, cold individuals incapable of empathy or warm emotional relating. They have been seen as self-centred, selfish, egocentric, self-obsessed and so on. It seems that there is a difficulty or misunderstanding in communicating the emotions in a way that makes sense to others. There is no doubt that Aspies have a personality aside from their diagnosis, and some individuals without doubt are egocentric, selfish and so on. However, in a general sense it seems that many Aspies have an extremely useful ability to remove themselves from the emotion in a situation where others may have difficulty in doing so. Being the person who can still see the logic whilst others may be distracted by emotion is a very powerful place to be.

Anyone looking for brave and stoical individuals? Look no further. We are constantly amazed at how strong-minded Aspies sometimes are. Stoicism is a marvellous trait of many people with Asperger's syndrome. It means being able to distance oneself from any number of emotional situations which are going on and to remain clear-minded and level-headed. This could help such an Aspie to get out of all sorts of potentially troubling situations. For example, if they see trouble coming, they simply don't get involved, which means that they stay safe and don't get into trouble themselves. The really positive thing about stoicism is that you can avoid taking sides. Being stoical doesn't mean that an Aspie is cold and uncaring, but more simply that they don't get blinded by emotion. One situation where this could be particularly useful is if a close relative has died and you are able to keep everything running smoothly while the rest of the family are too upset. In a job situation this sort of emotional detachment could be useful because you wouldn't get too emotionally involved in sensitive work where a family is dealing with a difficult situation and this could make you a real asset.

Chapter 5

Asperger's adults: Case studies

Since Asperger's syndrome is a condition which is highly individual, we felt it necessary to include the experiences and views of a variety of Aspie adults.

Case Study 1

Disability: A disadvantage or deficiency, especially a physical or mental impairment that interferes with or prevents normal achievement in a particular area.

Disorder: An ailment that affects the function of mind or body.

Name: Genevieve Edmonds

Age: 24

Age diagnosed with Asperger's syndrome (AS): 22

Do you have a formal diagnosis or self-diagnosed: Formal diagnosis

As an adult with AS do you agree that the condition is a disability/disorder?

My belief is that AS in itself is not a disorder or a disability. As soon as an AS individual enters a situation with the majority of other human beings the condition often becomes a disability; unless those they are with have that extremely rare ability to get the most out of an AS individual without being judgmental. In my opinion, as long as society is inflexible and unsupportive (deliberately or non-deliberately) towards individuals with invisibly different ways of processing the world, the chance of becoming disabled is high. This may be very cynical, but humans are naturally programmed to fight for their own survival. When it comes down to it, it is possible that in many cases humans will only support the less-abled out of necessity for social acceptance or out of an emotional attachment of some kind. It appears easier to get away with not supporting the individuals who are invisibly different. More excuses can be made to withhold support from these individuals as their support needs are much more subtle to the eye, so that they can become more 'disabled' more easily.

Would you say that your mental health has suffered as an Aspie?

Yes, I would say without a doubt my mental health has suffered as a result of both diagnosed and undiagnosed 'mild' Asperger's syndrome. Pre-diagnosis in childhood I was very anxious at times, but very happy. This was perhaps the result of lacking self-awareness. In this sense my anxiety didn't make sense since I was blissfully unaware of the reality shared by my neurotypical peers and that I somehow couldn't always access it. At the age of around 12 – 13 the truth of this situation really hit me. A frequent feeling I had was a sense that my peers ' knew something I didn't: i.e. they could make sense of the social world in an innate way. Since that time, when I realised that I was different, I have never really been the same. I was putting in the intellectual energy I had into bravely facing that confusion and despair and hiding the 'terrible secret' I had – that I was ashamed that I couldn't relate with ease to the people and situations around me. The fact that I appeared sometimes sophisticated and articulate, almost socially skilled in some ways, my 'secret' was not believable, when in reality the person they thought I was, was simply an intellectual creation based upon a set of intricately observed and copied behaviours.

From age 12 onwards the depression began which I continue to struggle at times. My other key emotion from 12 onwards was anger. How could a girl from a supportive, loving family with so much about her be so inexplicably angry? Looking back now, my anger was centered around the fact that I put so much energy and effort into appearing 'normal'. What angered me was that the sheer effort I put in was not noted or appreciated by others (not that they should've known, but I didn't 'get' that at the time), since how can a person voice such a phenomenon? How can one admit to such a crazy phenomenon, how can one find the words to describe such a thing? It's not something that is easily dropped into conversation is it, 'Oh by the way, I actually don't know how to make friends, why I should have them, when I have them, what to do with them, how I relate to anyone including my parents and teachers and how to make sense of most social situations.' All that despite having a great background and loving family. Knowing nothing about autism or Asperger's syndrome, it is unsurprising that I kept it to myself, blaming others and worst of all myself for the person who I was.

By age 18, I had learnt to numb my emotions for fear of losing total control. I was on auto-pilot most of the time, between outbursts of anger, anxiety, panic and temper, yet never losing hope that somehow things would get better...when... By the time I went to university the change in structure really hit home. The 'get better whens' were beginning to dry up the older I got, and things still hadn't changed. I found it at times impossible to cope even with a very structured school and home life, so the change to university was too much to bear. A year into university I was diagnosed as being clinically depressed and anxious which lasted a while culminating in an eventual nervous breakdown. Six months later I was diagnosed as having mild Asperger's syndrome.

I firmly believe my mental ill-health pre-diagnosis was brought about by lacking the knowledge of the condition with which to express myself and ask for help. Self-blame, ignorance and shame of the way I was led me to bottling it up. Having such a supportive and loving family meant that I could just about hold things together until I left for university so my issues were not seen in their true context.

Post-diagnosis my mental health has suffered in the sense of going through a grieving process which I hope will end soon. That is, the person I believed I was, or hoped I could become through sheer hard work, has not materialised. Perhaps this person will materialise in the future, who knows? I have been told it will but that I will reach that place in an unconventional way. I hope that this is to be true. Looking back I have some regret and anger, not with anyone but myself with all the effort I put in to appear 'normal'. I assumed that everyone had to put that degree of mental energy into relating to the world, and wondered how others could manage multiple other things such as studying, hobbies, a social life and so on. I could only cope with one thing at a time, which didn't really get me anywhere. If I had known what the problem was I might have been able to put my effort into areas I could have excelled in. The one area I did try to excel in, 'social and emotional relating', I now realise didn't and wouldn't win me any prizes. Looking back I wish I could've voiced how I felt since I had so much love and support around me. I didn't know there was such a condition for how I was! Getting over this is hard and this has led to an underlying depression which at present antidepressant drugs control well enough most of the time to keep me going.

What strategies would you recommend to other adult Aspies to stay mentally well?

● Medication

The levels of anxiety experienced by many Aspies are unacceptably high. High levels of anxiety, left untreated, whether their origins are organic or social, are liable to cause disability or worse still mental illnesses. Anxiety can hamper the ability to think through things in ways which are helpful or rational. For an Aspie, it is hard enough having to work through many areas of life intellectually, yet when hampered with anxiety affecting this coping skill things can become unbearable. It is a shame that sometimes medication is the only helpful way to keep anxiety levels down. I wish I did not have to rely on chemical input to keep me at a level of basic coping. I wish I could rely on nature to do this, but from experience this is not so in the 'real world'. Not right now anyway.

- Keep communicating

It was only after my diagnosis that I realised I perhaps lacked a natural understanding of communication that others seemed to have, which went beyond being introverted or shy. I hadn't known previously exactly when to communicate with others or why. I copied others around me assuming that that was what everyone did, not realising always what I was doing. Very often it just didn't occur to me to share what I was thinking with others or why. However, it is essential to keep communicating. I used to assume sometimes that others knew what was going on inside my head, as though they were psychic. What I didn't realise was that others could tell some things from my outside appearance but not everything. Therefore, when depressed or anxious, talk it out. Don't keep it in. People can't read your mind, and by the time you are already unwell mentally, the damage may have been done. If talking to someone is uncomfortable or unnatural for you, write down how you are feeling.

- Exercise

When I do it, I feel so much better. It makes me much less anxious, happier and more balanced. Try as hard as you can to exercise as much as possible. The problem sometimes for me is that when I am not functioning well, usually through anxiety or sensory overload, I need the support to go to the gym or go out walking. I am ashamed to ask for such support and feel that if I did ask, would it be given? Discomfort around being with others, in crowds or having to participate in social interaction of some kind which requires hard work for me and is anything but relaxing, such as in a walking group or going swimming, means that I often exclude myself from getting as much exercise as I would like. It is not motivation to do exercise that is the issue, it is going out into an often overwhelming world to do it.

- Learn strategies to channel anger positively

No matter how angry you feel at constant injustices, lack of respect, poor treatment and bullying behaviour, don't lose your temper. Remembering that the majority of the world not only have no motivation to accept different ways of thinking, they especially will not accept displays of anger, no matter how legitimate they are. If you have great anger with others, showing it in a way that is perceived as negative by the majority will often backfire on you. Channel it into ways which are positive. This is indeed easier said than done, and these channels are not always accessible. However, an angry outburst may last for a short while but the after-effects on others last much longer and are less easily forgotten or accepted, especially by NTs.

● Be self-reliant for happiness

Don't rely on others to make you happy. Becoming your own best friend is less clichéd than it sounds. Always look within to find happiness first of all. Happiness that comes from others should be looked on as a bonus, but not be relied upon.

● Have regular access to a place where you can be 'you'

Trying hard to access the NT majority world all the time is exhausting and hard work. Find a place or people with whom you can be 'you' without having to try too hard to appear 'normal' or 'acceptable' to others. In my case it is among nature and animals, especially horses. Wherever that may be, be it with other Aspies, a special interest or wherever, find it and do it often to re-energise yourself so you can face the world again.

● Ensure that you have 'refuelling' time

If you become regularly overloaded, it may be that you need regular 'refuelling' time where you may sleep more, need a controlled sensory environment and so on. I have noticed that many Aspies experience overload much more readily and so to avoid outbursts, anger, aggression or depression it is essential to retreat to a safe place when these signs start showing.

Please outline the attributes, your individual expression of AS, which you find positive

It is extremely hard to know what attributes are due to AS and what are simply personality. Or both. However, these are some attributes that may be AS based:

● Compassion

I have a very strong sense of compassion which goes beyond basic emotion. My compassion is based strongly upon my own experiences rather than empathy for empathy's sake, or for an empty reason lacking in true feeling such as social acceptance. My compassion leads me, when well, to possess a fierce sense of social justice especially with regards to individuals who are discriminated against in minority positions in society and those suffering from mental illnesses or differences. I refuse to accept social injustices for others who share the notion 'that is just the way the world works'. I refuse to abandon my viewpoint when faced with the plight of the underdog, namely those with hidden disabilities or those disabled by society. Much of this I keep to myself for fear of losing this attribute when faced with others who accept inequalities more readily.

- Devotion and dedication

If I do something I try to do it properly and thoroughly. This applies especially to personal relationships and friendships.

- Strong desire to be unjudgmental

I refuse to make emotionally based judgments about others. I am 'evidence-based' when it comes to assessing others so will not make any judgment until I have a large amount of factual evidence with which to do it. It seems that I cannot 'compute' making snap emotional judgments about social situations or people. This of course can lead some Aspies to becoming vulnerable to unscrupulous individuals and so is exercised with caution; however, it is a quality I am proud of. It means that I do not follow the crowd when making judgments that are often deeply unfair and discriminatory to others. I cannot bear to witness this.

Please outline (as briefly as possible!) your vision for AS adults in the future

My vision is idealistic. It concerns social diversity as a whole. I would like to see global acceptance and inclusion of individuals with mental differences (such as neurological or developmental differences) or disorders/disabilities, including individuals with mental illnesses. I would like to see the sort of discrimination of visibly disabled individuals, which at present is frowned at by the majority, translated to individuals with invisible differences/disabilities. I would like to see more responsibility being taken by society to eradicate the exclusion, ignorance and discriminatory practice so widely condoned at present. I want society to make individuals accountable who mindfully or through ignorance create a poor quality of life for these individuals. I would like a so-called civilised society to be made fully responsible to ensure that all individuals with a mental difference or illness are made equal members of society, as respected and valued human beings.

Please offer from your own experience your three top tips for other Aspies for getting the best out of themselves in adulthood

1. Don't be swayed by others who claim to talk for the Asperger's community. Never forget your own individuality and personality. Look to other Aspies for advice and support, but do so only in a context that makes sense to you as a person. Get to know you, not who you think you are or should be based on others who may have the same syndrome. We are simply individuals who share similar characteristics.

2. Don't accept poor treatment from individuals who are prejudiced, negative and ignorant of AS. You may not necessarily be able to change these individuals or their mindsets as after all, some people are simply too selfish to care, hence as I am often told, 'It's their problem, not yours.' However, learn to stand up for yourself and your needs as much as possible. Learn to become assertive and remove passivity and aggression from yourself. This is hard for individuals who may lack social knowledge or confidence but assertiveness can be faked to some degree.

3. Learn to articulate yourself and your needs in a clear and rational way. If you find that you articulate yourself better in writing or through an advocate, assert your right to do this. Speech does not have to be the only acceptable way to communicate.

Case Study 2

Name: Dean Worton

Age: 32

Age diagnosed with Asperger's syndrome (AS): 28

Do you have a formal diagnosis or self-diagnosed: Formal diagnosis

As an adult with AS do you agree that the condition is a disability/ disorder?

I'm not sure if there is a single person alive who has the definitive answer to whether AS is a disability or disorder. I believe that to be able to answer this question, you need to be able to define the terms disability and disorder, which I think is down to a number of separate interpretations. I guess it really depends on what point of view an individual is observing from. Perhaps the word disorder is closer to my own reality than the word disability because disorder could simply be used to describe the state of a different 'presentation' style of individual attributes when compared to the norm as opposed to the more clinical sense in which the term is more likely to be used in the same sentence as Asperger's syndrome.

If I do see Asperger's syndrome as a disorder this certainly doesn't mean that I see it as a wrongness, but rather by looking at it in the sense that a group of people have come together to create a jigsaw and we are not putting all of the pieces in the right places. However, from my personal point of view, it doesn't seem like a very democratic society if those people see fit to 'impose' upon everyone where the pieces are supposed to go and the problem is that the majority of people put most of the pieces in the right places and therefore its only when someone puts too many pieces in the wrong places that criticism is made by these people who seem to believe that they are wiser. So, in my own opinion, AS is only a disorder in the sense of not quite fitting but certainly not by any clinical definition of the term.

I'm not sure if it's an accurate portrayal to say that everyone with Asperger's syndrome has a disability. I would certainly agree that some people with Asperger's syndrome could be said to have a disability but the condition is so often intertwined with other conditions which are often undiagnosed that it's not always easy to know what is caused by Asperger's syndrome and what is caused by something else. Perhaps you could say that having significant cognitive difficulties is a disability, but then I don't know if everyone with AS has cognitive difficulties. It may even be that such problems suggest a co-occuring condition and not Asperger's syndrome. Therefore, it does seem a grey area as to whether AS can accurately be classed as a disability or whether in some individual cases of AS their only problem is that the way they are contradicts the way society as a whole wants people to be, when in fact if they lived in a foreign country or a few centuries ago the same behaviour might be the norm, which I think this boils down to the fact that Aspies are only disabled as a matter of opinion, but it just happens to be the opinion of the majority which is hardly surprising when the majority are so similar in their approach to life and their beliefs.

Would you say that your mental health has suffered as an Aspie?

There were two periods in my life when I allowed potential career and relationship opportunities to slip through the net simply through brief moments of bad judgment. As there was no way to salvage these particular opportunities and similar ones were rare, I did feel at the time that the quality of my life was unlikely to ever be as great as it might have been if it wasn't for letting my guard down on these two occasions and I did feel quite depressed at the time.

However, they were the type of scenarios that I can imagine most people have been through and although I would say that having AS caused the situations to arise, my reaction to these situations was possibly no different to those of an average person. Apart from those periods, I have always been a happy-go-lucky type individual with a positive outward outlook on life. I just take it as it comes and get on with it.

Throughout my university days, I had very limited social contact and of course as a result felt bored much of the time and would have liked slightly more social contact than the very small amount I had, yet for the most part, I managed to find solace in my own solitary way. I was doing a course which I thoroughly enjoyed and found hours of happiness learning new things about the subject and writing essays and reports, particularly in the foreign language subjects.

I spent a year of my course studying in France. I had limited contact with my French classmates, similar to my experience in the UK. However, I did not get downhearted about it. At worst I felt bored but this was counterbalanced by the sheer joy of listening to the tutor speaking away in

French listening to the students replying in French even when I didn't enjoy the particular subject being taught.

I recall one occasion when I had had a setback in my career and thought that I wasn't ever going to have a successful career. I had been patient for years throughout quite a variety of setbacks in my life and this time could quite easily have been the point where my patience had finally run out. Then the next day something happened that I could never have imagined which changed my life forever. Fittingly it was in January 2000, which has meant that the twenty-first century has been a very positive one for me because this is when my mother explained to me about an unknown 'condition' called Asperger's syndrome. Fortunately she saw the positives of it and said that it doesn't mean that something is wrong with me but just that Asperger's syndrome makes people's minds work in a different way and that for all anyone knows it could be that it's the Aspies that are right and the neurotypicals that are wrong.

Once I had had a chance to take all of this in, I started to feel far more positive. Even though at that time I didn't know if I would ever have a successful career, at least I knew the reason that my life hadn't seemed to move forward as much as other adults in their mid-twenties. Also, understanding myself more has allowed me to take control of my life and make it more positive. Things don't happen overnight, but even when things weren't necessarily going as well for me as they were for others my age, I just enjoyed what things were going well and since then my career and relationships have gone well.

What strategies would you recommend to other adult Aspies to stay mentally well?

● Eating a healthy diet

It helps me to eat lots of fruit and vegetables every day. Far from thinking it's boring, I actually feel happier because I feel fitter. Of course, doing this seven days a week would become very tedious so my strategy is to eat slightly more snack foods at the weekend.

● Getting exercise

If you can't face going to a gymnasium then you can always do some simple exercise in the privacy of your own home. Better still do it to music and if you're home alone why not close the curtains and dance to it? What harm can it do if no one else can see what you're doing?

- Listening to mood music

  For example, celtic music or the sounds of trees and waterfalls. It works wonders for me.

- Keeping occupied

  I truly believe that after leaving university, I managed to keep sane through a combination of voluntary work and studying. The great thing about voluntary work is that you can stay confident because you should only be expected to do what you're happy with and if you make a mistake it doesn't matter too much because there is no formal job description and the employer will just appreciate your help even if you only do an hour a month. Plus, it's great on CVs.

- Walking outside for at least twenty minutes every day

  A long country walk among beautiful scenery can be an amazing way to feel good. Somehow, it just seems to release any stress that you had been feeling. For those who don't mind crowds as much, you might enjoy visiting a city or small town. If you're confident enough to do so you could maybe arrange your own holiday to somewhere you've always wanted to go perhaps through the Internet as long, as you are realistic about safety.

- Joining a group which involves something that interests you

  Or maybe even pursuing a brand new hobby.

Please outline the attributes of your individual expression of AS which you find positive

The positive attribute that stands out as the most obviously Asperger-related is my ability to remember things that the majority of people simply would not remember. When I was at school, I knew the birthdays of everyone in my class and even knew the name of everyone in the year below me. I can also still remember the dates of minor events, which happened to me possibly as much as twenty years ago. I have always been good at remembering people's telephone numbers and addresses, and this has caused people to turn to me if they needed this information and it saved them from having to spend several minutes or more looking for it. This has proved particularly useful in my career because I've worked with data a lot.

I find it positive that I have a high aptitude for certain learning experiences. In particular, I am good at learning foreign languages and can speak French fluently, have a good command of German and picked Spanish up very quickly. I am also very good with certain computer applications and almost by default have become the database administrator in almost every organisation that I have worked for.

The other attributes that I find positive are loyalty and dedication. If I start something I always see it through. I think this is demonstrated by the fact that I hated computers when I was at school and found them excessively difficult and have completely turned this around. I love learning new facts about how things work and can become quite enthusiastic over it. Once I remember something I never forget, even when it takes me a long time to learn it in the first place. If I visit a new country, I try to find out what I can about its culture and this helps me to thoroughly enjoy the experience. When I meet new people, whether in my own country or abroad, I always take an interest in what they tell me. People often confide in me about things because I'm a good listener and they know I won't tell anyone else.

I am very patient and perseverant. I've rarely knocked back an invitation to a party because, while I often sat down for two hours without anyone speaking to me, eventually someone has. Then I'll come out of my shell and am rather more outgoing than the silent character from earlier in the night.

I have a very unique sense of humour. I'm not sure if everyone appreciates it but I think people sometimes find it refreshing and often think I'm funny.

Please outline your vision for AS adults in the future

My vision for AS adults in the future is that they should be able to benefit from a social and welfare system where the rules are changed in such a way that the needs of all individual members of society can be met without anyone having to declare themselves as disabled. As such, people with AS would be able to seek assistance with whatever they find difficult without having to apply through government departments and actually feeling disabled. I would like to see a service where if you need something doing there is an organisation that is able to do this for you without any fuss and that they treat their customers with respect and as equals.

The support could be made available in all areas of life from support into and during employment to independent living and social situations and easy access to training courses which help people with AS. This could be run alongside any NT's that may have difficulty with some of these things, and be tackled in a non-patronising way where everyone is treated with equal respect.

I would like Aspies to have more pro-active help to meet others like them so that they feel less unique, but also help to feel accepted in their jobs and community. I would like there to be sufficient public awareness of AS so that people adapt accordingly instead of making the person with AS feel uncomfortable by noticeably going out of their way to help them. In other words, to see an alternative way rather than be prescriptive about what is considered normal.

Please offer, from your own experience, your three top tips for other Aspies for getting the best out of themselves in adulthood?

1. Stay organised

   Just little things like taking five minutes out to tidy your living area every day can help other things to fall in place, making other chores seem like less hassle and making you feel happier and more confident. I listen to soothing music whilst doing this which means I can feel relaxed while getting things done.

2. Remember that you have as much right to be here as anyone else

   We are all born for a reason. I have never taken the negative outlook on life and don't let feelings of jealously towards NT's get the better of me. My basic outlook is that 'no one is better than me'. I have worked hard to integrate into society and people have come to see my qualities, even people who were more sceptical at first. Anyone who ridicules you has a problem themselves and a lack of information about AS.

3. Persevere

   I have kept sane by being a student in some way, shape or form until the age of thirty and obtained several qualifications which have been helpful in my career. I have also been involved in voluntary work which has not only increased my employment skills but has helped me to meet many new and interesting people and become confident and fairly outgoing (I wasn't previously). Not many of these positive experiences were immediate but I kept trying and got there in the end and have achieved success in my career and relationships. Sometimes, I felt like I didn't have the energy to pursue some tiring and time-consuming endeavours but I kept the momentum and it's all been well worth it. Even if I hardly have any free time, I enjoy everything I do.

Case Study 3

Name: Giles Harvey

Age: 30

Age diagnosed with Asperger's syndrome (AS): 22

Do you have a formal diagnosis or self-diagnosed: I now have a formal diagnosis of Asperger's syndrome, but was originally self-diagnosed.

As an adult with AS do you agree that the condition is a disability/disorder?

Asperger's syndrome is only a disability if it is made to feel like a disability. I don't really regard myself as having a disorder. The terminology I prefer to use is that it is merely a difference from being neurotypical. AS shouldn't be treated like a handicap. People with Asperger's syndrome can, and do, very many positive and worthwhile activities and lead as full and as active lives as possible.

Would you say that your mental health has suffered as an Aspie?

My mental health has suffered from time to time. As someone with Asperger's syndrome, I suppose my mental health declined as for a long time I had no role. I became anxious and depressed, along with very many other Asperger's diagnosed people that are out there. My mental health also suffered because I wanted to achieve the same goals as neurotypical people around me. The role model of the nice young male or female who has lots of friends, marries the nice partner, has a good job and has two or three nice children, a nice home and a nice car, was an aim that most people had and I wondered why I wasn't achieving any of this.

I think the pressure society seems to put people under, having come to terms with my Asperger's syndrome, isn't necessary. We live in a busy fast flowing world, which has many hidden problems under the surface. Because someone is perceived as being successful it doesn't necessarily mean they don't have difficulties and that life is a breeze; they equally have hard day-to-day problems.

I still have down days or periods when everything is negative, but eventually my positivity wins through because I want it to win through.

What strategies would you recommend to other adult Aspies to stay mentally well?

I think that success, in terms of staying mentally well (as someone with Asperger's syndrome) is about staying occupied and about being creative if you can. It's also about making an effort to motivate yourself and trying to meet other similar people. As a first step, never be afraid to try new things – I only learnt to play the piano at age twenty-six. I didn't do it to take exams and I am not a wonderful pianist, but I enjoy the feeling I get when I play a nice piece of music well. Other people I know get satisfaction through art, computers or outdoor activities.

Meeting Aspies and being in a support group is also useful, as you can relate to other's experiences and share advice and understanding of one another. Some Aspies also go on to become best of friends and partners through meeting others rather than staying isolated. Another focus to wellbeing is making sure that all the medication you are prescribed by your doctor is taken, to the exact quantity stated, even when you feel well, as moods and situations can easily deteriorate.

Keeping your mind occupied gives less opportunity to dwell on negative problems and experiences. Quite often, it is only when you do this that bigger aims like relationships and work may work out. Use any free time as time to discover yourself, your abilities and your needs.

Generally, in terms of good mental health, there is a three way input – medication, activity and therapy – in order to start to become well. Avoid examining neurotypical people's successes too much as this can have a negative effect. Try to remember everyone is different and that everyone has down and up days. If I was highly successful I very much doubt I could cope with the higher pressure problems that would be placed on me, as my coping mechanism would be less able to adapt. Try also to remember that not all neurotypical people are successful. Plenty of neurotypical people can be shy, lonely and out of work too.

Please outline the attributes your individual expression of AS which you find positive?

My willingness to try and never give up. I believe my staying power at things is very positive. It has only been through my sheer determination that I have achieved many of the skills I have, such as swimming, cycling, driving, friendship, work and gaining formal qualifications. As someone with Asperger's syndrome the ability to persevere and not give up certainly helps, despite all the difficulties that I have faced reaching these targets.

My ability to be creative and express myself through the hobbies I have and to drive away from situations that have stressed me have also helped. As I have mentioned previously, I read, play the piano and use my computer both to search the Internet and write and record data for my hobbies. I also speak about Asperger's syndrome to gain the benefit of helping other people similar to myself; this gives me a real boost. Driving is another passion of mine, it allows me to get about and discover new, exciting, interesting places; in fact my car probably does about 15,000 miles per year, much of this being pleasure mileage. Often when I feel down, this helps lift the way I feel. The car also gives me a feeling of responsibility, in terms of safety of other road users and pedestrians, and also maintenance and looking after the documentation required to run a car. It's also surprising how many interesting places there are in England, Scotland and Wales that I have come across. I also find map reading enjoyable and this certainly helps me navigate the United Kingdom.

I enjoy meeting and helping the many people with Asperger's syndrome who perhaps don't have as much life experience as me. It may be company or advice about how to act in a certain situation that they are looking for, but it certainly gives me a sense of achievement and self-satisfaction.

Please outline (as briefly as possible!) your vision for AS adults in the future?

My hope for adults with Asperger's syndrome in the future is that more of us will be able to work, run our own homes and find partners, but in reality this may not be possible. Opportunities to socialise, study, work, train and gain other worthwhile skills increases this possibility. I would like more people with Asperger's syndrome to get to know one another and share experiences and pass on expertise. Hopefully, people with Asperger's syndrome can, in future, live as fulfilling lives as possible. I also think that creativity and exercise will increase people's wellbeing and confidence, perhaps to the point that they can try out some of the more vital lifestyle skills required to work, look after a home and meet others.

Maybe technology can provide some solutions to developing services for adults with Asperger's syndrome. We already know the benefits that the internet has provided for some people with Asperger's syndrome. It is perfectly possible that by taking this concept one step further these links have the possibility of being strengthened maybe by using video technology to aid the ability of people with Asperger's syndrome to actually see and talk to one another without even leaving the home. Technological innovation also means home working opportunities could become an option for people with Asperger's syndrome, which means that flexible hours and a more comfortable working environment become much more of a possibility. In turn, this will hopefully have a positive effect in increasing the number of people with Asperger's syndrome with employment opportunities.

Please offer, from your own experience, your three top tips for other Aspies for getting the best out of themselves in adulthood?

1. Keep busy and stay occupied

   By staying occupied you have less opportunity to dwell on the bad points of life, such as failure to achieve a social goal. There are many ways people with Asperger's syndrome can stay busy. Hobbies that involve creative input can be especially good, such as art, music and drama. I have found playing the piano especially advantageous to me. The piano is thought to be beneficial for people with Asperger's syndrome as it improves hand and eye co-ordination, doesn't need an orchestra to play with so therefore communication isn't important, and can offer a feeling of achievement. Activities that involve exercise have other benefits in that they pump oxygen into the brain, and relieve the brain's stresses. Walking is especially beneficial as are other non-competitive sporting activities, such as horse riding, swimming, cycling and jogging.

2. Change the mindset

   Try not to focus on past events and failure. Try to be positive, always look to the rest of today and the future, because yesterday and earlier today have gone, and what's done is done. Try also to value any achievements that you have made, particularly those that few others have, or those that are rare for people with Asperger's syndrome to achieve. These could include skills such as gaining academic or professional qualifications, learning to drive, meeting a partner, performing on a musical instrument in front of an audience, gaining a job or buying a first home. Try also to learn skills from neurotypical people by watching and analysing how they behave in various situations and then translate this to your own circumstances.

   See any mistakes, no matter how humiliating or embarrassing they have been, as a learning curve. Learn from them and try to ensure that you don't make the same mistakes again. Learn from others what you did wrong and convert this into knowledge for the future. Mistakes can be quite valuable, no one should be afraid of making them as these are a way of learning life skills.

3. Meet and share experiences with other Aspies

    One of the main benefits to my quality of life has been meeting with and
    sharing experiences with other people who have Asperger's syndrome.
    Many people who have Asperger's syndrome are sympathetic to the
    situations that fellow Aspies can find themselves in and will happily
    share experiences or pass on knowledge to one another. Other Aspies
    also make valuable friends and companions.

    There are a few different ways to fellow Aspies. These include joining
    a social or leisure group for people with Asperger's syndrome. Several
    exist around the country and if you live in the United Kingdom your
    nearest one can be found by checking out the PARIS website of the
    National Autistic society. You could also join a website for people with
    Asperger's syndrome, some of which are listed within this guide –
    otherwise use a search engine to find one you like. Some groups arrange
    meet-ups for members and this is an opportunity to meet other similar
    people. The other way could be to have an Aspie pen-pal and write
    letters or send e-mails to one another.

case study

Case Study 4

Name: E Veronica (Vicky) Bliss

Age: Do we really need to know this?!

Age diagnosed with Asperger's syndrome (AS): Not diagnosed – just suspected!

As an adult with AS (characteristics) do you agree that the condition is a disability/disorder?

I see many people with AS in my capacity as a solution-focused psychologist, and without doubt, they are the most creative, sensitive, kind and funny people I have ever met. It is my privilege and pleasure to meet and work with them. The 'disability' aspect of AS comes from neuro-typical people who are not able to be flexible enough to appreciate the unique strengths and lovely character of people with AS. If the majority of people did not insist that everyone was the same, people with AS would not stand out as 'disabled' or 'disordered'.

I like the notion that AS is a 'difference' rather than disorder or disability and I would be pleased to see that more professionals were taking up this stance. I have been reading well-written, well-researched, and well-regarded books about autism where hundreds of pages have been devoted to describing the details of just how disabled people with autism are. Crikey, I felt like blowing my head off after the first few chapters. Other books however, especially those written from personal viewpoints, which are also well-written, well-researched but not I think as well-regarded are a pleasure to read. It is clear that the disabling part of autism is in the minds of the professional authors when one compares the two types of books.

I have noticed that 'normal' people are quite disabled sometimes by their emotions. Apparently some people are more concerned with knowing whether or not I like them than they are with listening to what I am saying. I had no idea about this, but once I knew it, it cleared up a lot of odd things that 'normal' people were doing. I thought these people were cognitively handicapped when it turns out their brains were just processing information differently from mine.

Sometimes people with autism have special talents and they are called 'savants' because of this. From my point of view 'normal' people appear to be 'social savants'. That is to say that they have especially good skills at talking to everyone (though not necessarily to convey information) and when one is in the room with a 'social savant' one can be sure to have a drink and something to nibble and the house will be clean and well-organised. Other examples of the savant skills of 'normal' people include the ability to plan meals, prepare them in advance, and time their cooking so everything gets done at once. These are just examples of some of their special skills. Their disabilities appear to be a tendency to take illogical decisions based on emotion rather than facts, and a tendency to read too much into what other people say rather than listen literally to the information. They concentrate on odd things, like make-up, hair style and matching clothing and are keen to make their outside look good, often appearing to neglect the substance inside themselves which is quite important too. They want to be seen doing the right things and seen to do good. People with autism actually want to be good. They want to be true to themselves first, and worry about pleasing others later.

For a long time now, the principles of 'normalisation' have guided care in the community for people with autism – though not necessarily for people with AS, who often get no care in the community. This is the idea that paid care staff have the job of helping people with autism 'fit in' to their local community. Staff were supposed to help people with autism participate in their community, with socially valued roles, real choices, and a positive presence in the community. The idea was to make disabled people look and behave as normally as possible, so the 'regular' folk could tolerate and like them. This is wrong on so many levels and I would prefer to have had the focus on paid staff helping people with autism be just who they were whilst also helping the community loosen their grip on what they considered 'acceptable' behaviour.

In the main then, I think people with autism do not have a 'thing' called disability. Their behaviours are judged disabled by 'normal' people. Normal people, on the other hand, have behaviours which are judged by autistic people as disabled. The difference is that 'normal' people are in the majority, so their view most often sticks.

Would you say that your mental health has suffered as an Aspie?

Again, I am not formally diagnosed as an Aspie, but becoming one is something I could aspire to! I do have many traits of an Aspie, and I can remember being in an almost perpetual state of wonder at the people around me as I was growing up. When I started school, I found other kids and teachers something of a mystery, but I assumed that other people were simply not as smart as me (!) so my mental health and self-esteem did not suffer. Through my teen years, I was very, very active and quite a perfectionist with music so I had very little time to think about myself or anyone else which was probably a good thing. I had many physical ailments however, such as headaches and stomach complaints, though no physical reason for these could ever be found.

When I went away to college, I continued with the type of lifestyle a psychologist would call 'manic'. I packed much into a short time and discovered the wonders of alcohol and caffeine. Again, I did not give myself much time for comparison of myself to other people, and usually when I did compare myself I came out favourably! Basically I felt that what I did made sense whereas other people were illogical. I was pretty self-contained in my own lovely little world.

I achieved my Bachelor of Arts degree with honours and worked as a social worker for adults with learning disabilities for five years before trying to return to university for a Master's Degree in Psychology. I received such kind support from the people with learning disabilities, their families and my colleagues during this time. I think now that because I was working side by side with people who were already labelled 'odd' I did not particularly stand out as different apart from perhaps my level of energy and the silly amount of alcohol I could drink and still go to work the next day. People also laughed a lot when they were with me, though I can remember not intending to be funny and not always understanding the jokes. I was glad people were happy to be with me and, completely without malice, laughed right along with them. When I wasn't physically ill, I remember this as a nice period in my life.

After five years as a social worker, I moved to a city where I didn't know anyone and I enrolled in the courses I needed in order to make a good application to the Master's programme in Psychology. There was no one there to support me or to fill in the gaps between my thinking and the workings of the 'real' world, and things rapidly fell apart. Panic attacks came with a vengeance and the only thing I used to counter act these was religion, to which I applied myself with vigour. I remember having no money for food because I gave my last dollar to the church. My brother constantly sent me money and I think he loaned me his car as well which was typical of his generosity and my need.

Eventually I was accepted into the Master of Arts programme in Counselling Psychology and found two mentors who were odd enough themselves to appreciate my straightforward honest-to-a-fault approach to things. However, I was under constant scrutiny from colleagues on the course and from teachers who were determined to dissect my psyche before turning me loose as a Counselling Psychologist.

I applied myself to the academic work with my usual manic enthusiasm, but was completely unprepared to receive statements and questions about my emotions and feelings. Tutors kept saying I was not 'in touch' with my emotions, that I was 'cold'; that I could not help other people until I 'worked through' my own past traumas. It seemed that whenever I asked a question, the tutor turned the spotlight on me and what it was about me that made me ask that particular question. I found myself actually wondering whether or not I had been abused as a child by some crazy uncle or town crank because other budding therapists and professors kept insisting it was odd that I didn't like social touch. Cue the onset of even more spectacular panic attacks, palpitations, dizzy spells, chronic colds and even hallucinations (but don't tell anyone about that will you? I certainly didn't until recently).

I used my course text books to diagnose myself, I hounded tutors for help with what was wrong with me, I saw psychologists, counsellors and a psychiatrist, though I was sensibly guarded in what I told them in terms of my symptoms. If I hadn't been guarded, that is, if I had told them of my hallucinations, I am sure I would have been hospitalised with some serious sounding psychiatric disorder. I was prescribed Prozac, but decided not to take it. I stopped eating, applied myself even more to academic study seeking desperately to understand what was wrong with me and, quite bizarrely, I got engaged to be married, thinking that I must be normal because this is what normal people did.

The addition of planning a wedding to my already demented schedule was the proverbial straw that broke the camel's back. I found myself making an appointment to see the university student counsellor because I was becoming debilitated by jumbled thoughts and forgetfulness and profound weepiness. I still was not eating and my course work was beginning to suffer which was an unacceptable state of affairs from my skewed point of view.

I remember hearing my name called when I was in the counsellor's waiting room, standing up and walking for what seemed like three days, whilst my shoes made this hideous noise on the tiled hallway, which seemed to have no end. It was the longest walk in my life and I was in tears before I even reached the office.

It was this man, whose name I am sorry to say I cannot recall, who asked me to do a little test, the results of which turned my sad little life around.

91

The test showed that only 3 % of the population thought like I did, and that the majority of people had brains that worked in a different way. Once I was armed with this information, I shared it with absolutely anyone who would listen. I talked in detail, with wide-eyed wonder, about how differently people thought from me. I was obsessed with this discovery – it still makes me smile to remember the relief of this bit of knowledge. It provided me with at least a little ammunition for those tutors and colleagues who continued to criticise me for not feeling more and for always 'intellectualising' things and above all, who made me feel distinctly inferior.

That was a long answer to a question about my mental health! I still would not say my mental state suffered because of Aspie traits, but because Aspie traits were not seen as acceptable by the majority of people around me. If everyone had been as accepting as my mother, for example, my mental health would not have suffered.

What strategies would you recommend to other adult Aspies to stay mentally well?

Work out who you are, even if who you are changes every day, and find ways to be just that so long are you are not hurting yourself or anyone else. You are a wonderfully unique person and you know yourself better than anyone. Listen to others critically, learn what you can, accept help graciously and make your own decisions.

Please outline the attributes, your individual expression of AS, which you find positive.

People say I am straight to the point: it always surprises me because I don't actually set out to be straight to the point, but there it is.

I have a sense of humour that really amuses me. Often I amuse others too, but mainly I make myself laugh and I really love that. For example, I buy bread with 'invisible crusts' because it amuses me to imagine sneaking up on a loaf to see if I can see the crust before it disappears. It is truly funny that someone, somewhere spent time working out how to make the crusts disappear! Invisible crusts… honestly, isn't the world a hilarious place?!

I am happy in my own company or with my animals. I feel safer if I don't need people because they are unpredictable, so I like being able to count on myself.

I seem to be able to encourage and to calm both people and animals.

I have a keen sense of right and wrong and am an excellent rule follower – so long as the rule makes sense.

I am an excellent rule-breaker when the need arises!

I am pretty good at learning from things I see which makes me a good observer and helps me help others.

I have a very strong desire to be 'useful' so if I see a way I can help people or animals I am happy to do so.

I do not like to be the centre of attention, so it is in my nature to attribute successes to the people and animals I am trying to help, which is how it should be.

I think a lot and try to understand things before I speak. I try to say what I mean and mean what I say, and I wish more people did this.

I do not require that people are 'normal' and I refuse to put pressure on people to conform.

Please outline (as briefly as possible!) your vision for AS adults in the future.

I would like to see AS people take over the world! It would be a much more logical, sensible place and probably no one would litter. I hate litter.

Please offer from your own experience your three top tips for other Aspies for getting the best out of themselves in adulthood.

1. Take credit for knowing and liking yourself.

2. Be as kind as you can be to people and animals.

3. Don't litter, flush and always wash your hands.

Case Study 5

Name: Judy Berkowicz

Age: 56

Age diagnosed with Asperger's syndrome (AS): 52

Do you have a formal diagnosis or self diagnosis: I do have a formal diagnosis. I decided to have the diagnosis as I have a son with AS and my daughters often said I showed many of the same traits that he has.

As an adult with AS do you agree that the condition is a disability/ disorder?

I like to look at having AS as an inconvenience rather than as a disability. It is useful to define it as a disability in order to claim benefits or any support that may be required. I think it is often NTs who look on AS as a disability as I tend to behave in unusual ways at times. Just because I tend to do something in an unusual way does not mean that I have a disability.

Would you say that your mental health has suffered as an Aspie?

I have not had any serious mental health problems from being an Aspie. I often feel low and depressed by the fact that no one ever seems to understand where I am coming from. Not having any friends can make me often feel like I am worthless and not worth knowing.

I have always had difficulties with work, both finding it and holding down a job. This is very demoralising as I feel that I am as good as the next person but because of the way I act or speak I am perceived as being different. I am now in work and do need support. Most of my work colleagues, while not bullying me, hardly acknowledge I exist and usually only speak to me in connection with work. I am never invited to join any of them for lunch and that often makes me feel despondent.

I must admit that now that I am living on my own I do find it much easier to become depressed. When my children were growing up I found it easier to keep cheerful as they gave me a purpose.

What strategies would you recommend to other adult Aspies to stay mentally well?

I think that in order to stay mentally well it is important to try and keep busy. I now work three days a week and although, as mentioned previously, I do not have much interaction with my colleagues, the job is very important to me as it gives me a feeling of self-worth and that I also fit into the general community. I have had some problems lately and my job was under threat but I am hoping that with the support I get from Prospects it will become a permanent arrangement.

I am also doing an A level psychology course which helps to keep me mentally well although I often find it hard to get motivated to do the tasks set. I really enjoy the subject and find it fascinating and interesting. My confidence has just been boosted as I have passed the exams I took in January.

My computer is very important to me and often finding other Aspies to chat to online makes me realise there are other people like me around so I do not feel so alone.

It is also important to keep physically active. I enjoy walking and if I feel really low and down I will go for a walk even if it is just round the block. I find this helps clear my head and I am able to cope better. When my kids were little and I found the situation was too much for me I would go for a walk round the block and come back able to face them again.

It is also important to do ordinary everyday activities that everyone else does. I go shopping, go to the bank and when I go to work I travel on the tube. By doing these activities I am mingling with the general public and as far as they are concerned I am the same as every one else. This helps me to feel that I am not so different to NTs.

I try to find out as much as I can about AS and if people show an interest I am willing to talk about it.

Please outline the attributes your individual expression of AS which you find positive.

I think a positive attribute of having AS is that I have learned to cope on my own without having a dependence on other people. I have been on holidays on my own, or not exactly on my own in that I join groups, but on free days I am quite happy to go off and do my own thing if no one wants to join forces with me. When I go to visit any of my children, although I like to spend time with them, if they have other commitments I am so used to managing on my own and finding my way round places that I am not left at a loose end. I also enjoy reading, which I do with any spare time I have. I tell myself that I have as much right to be in this world as anyone else and that it is often the other people who have the problems. Not me.

I am reliable and punctual and hate it if I am prevented from reaching my destination on time.

Please outline (as briefly as possible) your vision for AS adults in the future.

I am hoping that people with AS will be seen to be a normal part of society and accepted for who they are and given the same chances as other people. We may sometimes need a bit of extra help and support but when given this support we can usually fit into society well. We are not the only members of society that often need that little bit of extra help. I am sure that there are times when NTs need help at sometime in their lives and no one makes them feel bad about needing the help.

I would also like NTs to recognise that most people with AS are intelligent even though their behaviour may sometimes give the opposite impression. We do not like being treated as if we are stupid and unable to comprehend what is going on.

I also hope that NTs will realise that people with AS are as varied a group as NTs and not all of them have obsessions.

The government also need to do more to help the general community become aware that people with AS can integrate well. More jobs for people with AS should be offered in the Civil Service and then maybe the general population will follow the Government's lead.

I would also like to see people with AS portrayed in the media as being able to fit into society. At the moment I often find that it is the negative points about AS or the over-exaggerated emphasis on their mathematical ability or extraordinary memory that are seen on TV programmes.

Please offer from your own experience your three top tips for other Aspies for getting the best out of themselves in adulthood.

1. Keep busy

   I find that it is important to try and keep busy and find something that I know I can do on my own if need be. I always try and get out of the house to get some exercise and fresh air. If possible also try to talk to people you meet such as sales assistants or people in a restaurant.

Unless you are rude to people you should receive a civilised reply. This gives you a chance to practice your inter-personal skills and in such a short conversation you come over as being normal.

2. Try out new skills

The world is a big place. Nowadays there are so many possibilities out there so try and find a new hobby that would interest you and possibly make new friends and acquaintances. I find that even though friendships do not develop out of the classroom, workplace etc., whilst there, having something in common with the other people around you means you are not in total isolation. I have sometimes found that suggestions I have made in these circumstances are listened to and taken as seriously as those by NTs in the group.

3. Try to have contact with other Aspies

I find that talking to other Aspies can have a positive result. We can discuss our problems and difficulties and help each other to resolve them. When meeting up with other Aspies it is easier to be myself as we all accept each other much more for who we are. I have been on one meet up from the Aspie site which I found very enjoyable and went very well.

Prospects also run a social twice a year for all the clients and staff. I find this useful and helpful as I learn ways people manage at work. Also the staff being around helps to make sure that the conversation keeps flowing and that no one feels left out. By going to these social evenings I have also found out that I am not the only one who has had difficulty finding and keeping work.

Case Study 6

Name: Mand Harrison

Age: 26

Age diagnosed with Asperger's syndrome (AS): 24

Do you have a formal diagnosis or self-diagnosed: self, followed up by formal

As an adult with AS do you agree that the condition is a disability/ disorder?

I do not believe that AS is a disability – I believe the condition is very much made up of a collection of both positive and negative traits, which, to me, overall does not make it a disorder. The world is full of many different types of people and I believe not only in tolerance of diversity (both mental and physical) but in embracing it. Having AS has blessed me in seeing the world in such a way that I have substantial talent in both the world of art and of science – an unlikely pairing, but a contrast in ways of thinking that I really enjoy.

So my thinking, dress sense, topics of conversation and sense of humour are unique, to say the least – but I have a good job, I drive my own car and I live in a nice house with my husband. There are of course certain situations in life that I struggle with, but looking at the bigger picture, there really is no major problem in the scheme of things.

Would you say that your mental health has suffered as an Aspie?

I cannot deny that this was an issue in the past, prior to diagnosis and previous to ever having heard of this condition. As a younger child I didn't really care about being different as I wasn't fully aware of the effects of relationships with other people.

As I entered my teenage years I was torn apart because I didn't enjoy the same things as my peers, such as secretly smoking cigarettes on the far side of the school field or getting drunk in pubs every weekend. There were times when my small friendship group would turn against me and this began the first of several periods of depression. I felt very alone in the world, I was stuck in my bedroom and believed that nobody liked me – but at the same time I felt it was wrong to join in the group's behaviour in order to be accepted.

Consequently throughout my teens I saw many doctors, psychiatrists and counsellors in a bid to discover the source of discord that was constantly present in the background of my life. GPs would just send me on my way with a box of anti-depressants and specialists would interrogate me, searching for some deeply hidden childhood trauma that simply never existed.

At one stage I was diagnosed with 'a precursor to bi-polar disorder' that 'may or may not develop into the condition' with time. The psychiatrist said that because my moods were up and down so rapidly, there would be little point in offering medication.

In my early twenties, upon discovering Aspergers on *Newsround* one day, I suddenly felt I had found the answer I had been searching for. However, when I put forward my case to the consultant, she quashed my ideas – stating that I could speak perfectly well and therefore couldn't possibly have Aspergers or any other communication disorder. This unexpected knock back saw me into another period of depression as I felt I was so close to working out who I was.

It was another two years before I was finally sent to CLASS (an AS diagnostic clinic in Cambridge) and had my suspicions confirmed. Diagnosis was the positive turning point in my life which made sense of my life and ended my years of intermittent depression.

What strategies would you recommend to other adult Aspies to stay mentally well?

I think the most important thing is to make the effort to really understand and accept your condition, so that you do not have to fight against it all the time. I no longer force myself into situations in order to please other people, but at the same time I realise that to maintain any relationship you have to give and take.

As soon as I got used to the idea that I had AS it was my decision then to share this discovery with all of my friends. Now the people who know me understand, for example, that I don't like speaking on the phone and that it's not me being ignorant, it is my preference to keep in touch by text and email, which generally is not a problem.

From my own experience I believe that taking anti-depressants is very serious and should only ever be considered as a last option when you feel you have tried every other route. I'm not saying that they aren't useful on a short-term basis for certain individuals, rather that it probably isn't wise for GPs to hand them out as a matter of course without making real efforts to address the cause of a patient's negative thoughts and feelings.

I strongly recommend finding out about positive thinking techniques – these are simple methods using flashcards throughout the day to replace your negative thought patterns with new positive ones. Seems too good to be true? Try it, you will start to feel happier and more confident in no time! Just search online for 'positive affirmations' and you can begin retraining your subconscious mind and breaking out of the negative mental habits that held you down in the past.

Please outline the attributes your individual expression of AS which you find positive

I believe my positive attributes far outweigh the negative and to write about them all would take up a whole book of its own. Here are just some:

(a) My photographic memory. This has enabled me to learn and retain information with minimal tuition.

(b) Painting and drawing. A common feature on the autistic spectrum, which I do in my spare time for enjoyment and relaxation.

(c) Pedantry. Used sparingly at certain times this can provide amusement as opposed to mere factual correction.

(d) Idiosyncratic use of language. My own little quirks and unusual use of language amuses not just me but also those around me. I've noticed that other people start picking up on my made-up phrases which is another confirmation that they see such behaviours in a positive way.

(e) Diplomacy. I can always see the validity of both sides of a discussion. Doesn't help with my indecision, but it feels good to have an open mind.

(f) Being me. Now I am old enough to understand that it's OK to be an individual I am proud of the fact that I don't go against my personal beliefs just to please other people.

Please outline (as briefly as possible!) your vision for AS adults in the future

In a perfect world, all people would be open and understanding of others' needs, but of course, we are not living in a perfect world. The best we can hope for, realistically, is a raised awareness in society of not only people with AS but of all neurodiversity. These invisible differences go unseen by the world at large because it would be virtually impossible for every person on this planet to understand in any depth, all the hidden conditions that other people live with each day.

I would like to see more support for adults with AS who need it. Having looked into support groups for social skills assistance, I found these were few and far between and only available within office hours. This suggests to me that the general consensus is that people that are able to hold down full-time jobs do not require such support.

I guess a more positive, supportive approach from the medical profession would be a huge step forward. Nobody should have to endure knockbacks like the one I experienced with the consultant psychologist. That day I was made to feel like a fraud, like a stupid hypochondriac little girl with ideas above her station. I suppose this could only be addressed by increasing the number of specialist diagnosticians, which in turn would call for more support groups to help advise adults after diagnosis. Unfortunately there will always be limitations on such developments as there are so many conditions out in the world which need increased awareness and support. I believe that much of the work towards a brighter future for adults with AS comes from the AS community itself. With the aid of the Internet we are able to help ourselves and each other by forming communities in which we can find mutual ground. As long as we can avoid an 'us and them' mentality (between AS and NT) in these online communities, I believe that this will continue to be the best way forward.

Please offer from your own experience your three top tips for other Aspies for getting the best out of themselves in adulthood

1. Don't let irrational fears or lack of self-belief affect your life choices. If there are things you want to do with your life, don't write them off because you are in the habit of 'playing it safe'. With risk comes reward – often you will discover there was nothing to fear and the satisfaction you feel makes you wonder what you were waiting for.

2. Be yourself and trust yourself to make the right decisions. You are not in the playground any more so your friends will be mature enough to accept you for who you are. If they don't, they couldn't have been much of a friend in the first place.

3. Let the past be done. Don't waste time worrying over what has happened or what might have been. Life is a journey, rich with experiences, some positive and some negative – the important thing is that you learn from any mistakes you make along the way. You wouldn't keep reminding a good friend of their past mistakes, so be a friend to yourself and let it go. Enjoy your journey, I'm loving every moment of mine.

Case Study 7

Name: Mark Haggarty

Age: 27

Age diagnosed with Asperger's syndrome (AS): 26

Do you have a formal diagnosis or self-diagnosed: Initially self-diagnosed; later received a formal diagnosis.

As an adult with AS do you agree that the condition is a disability/disorder?

Yes. Because I lack certain abilities that neurotypical people generally possess, I am disadvantaged. In my mind, that constitutes a disability. I am disabled because of my inability to effectively engage in social pursuits with others. I am disabled because I cannot cope with some situations that others appear to handle with ease.

I feel perfectly comfortable considering myself as having a disability, and I don't see why any stigma should be associated with this. After all, it is not the fault of disabled individuals that they are the way they are.

I am very much aware that there are many individuals with Asperger's syndrome who vehemently assert that they are not disabled, and I can sort of understand why. I am also aware that some of these individuals find it offensive if someone suggests to them that they are disabled. To a large extent, I feel the opposite. If someone who supposedly knows that I have Asperger's syndrome was to suggest that I am not disabled, and that I should simply 'get a grip', I would be extremely annoyed.

I remember that the diagnostician who provided my diagnosis became apologetic when she realised that during the course of our discussions, she had referred to Asperger's syndrome as a disability. I assured her that nothing she had said had caused me to be offended, as I feel that Asperger's syndrome is indeed a disability.

There is the temptation to be dogmatic by attempting to prove one's point by analysing the definition of the terms 'disability' and 'disorder' in the dictionary, but I don't think that would make a very meaningful contribution to the debate. Each individual with Asperger's syndrome will have his or her own opinion on this issue which they will hold for their own reasons, and there is no reason why anyone has to be right or wrong. Whilst there is no harm in debating it, this is not a clear-cut subject and I believe that in the majority of cases, no amount of discussion will persuade anyone to deviate from their point of view.

In trying to provide an objective viewpoint, I have to consider that whilst neurotypical people have abilities that I do not, it is equally true that I have some abilities that the majority of neurotypicals appear to lack. Maybe it could be said that everyone is disabled in some way.

Would you say that your mental health has suffered as an Aspie?

I would say that this is the case. I think that the most notable factor which has led me to think so is the fact that I grew up undiagnosed. Had this not been the case, and had I known from an early age why I was different from other people, I might be giving a different answer to this question.

One thing that comes into my mind when I think about this are some famous words from a play by Jean-Paul Sartre: 'L'Enfer, c'est les autres.' Hell is other people. However unfruitful it may be to think in such a way, I have felt a certain affiliation with that quote ever since I first heard it, because for me it is so meaningful. Sartre stated that his quote was not meant to mean that one's relationships with other people are always poisoned; in fact it means that the way that we feel about ourselves is always influenced by the way that other people judge us. So if one's relationships with others are bad, then those other people can only be hell. I believe that the adverse affects on my mental health have been brought about not because of the simple fact that I have Asperger's syndrome, but by the way that other people have behaved towards me and treated me because I am different, in particular my peers during my school years. Their unsympathetic opinions of me have led to me having a low opinion of myself, which has left me with extremely low self-esteem.

Going through secondary school was particularly trying. The plights that I went through, which for me included the bullying and social isolation that many people with Asperger's syndrome sadly do suffer, I think were the biggest factors contributing to the adverse effects on my mental health. Admittedly my social isolation was in part self-inflicted; however, like many others with Asperger's syndrome, I have the tendency to refrain from putting myself in situations that I cannot cope with. One of the things that was particularly distressing was that I seemed to be something of a bully magnet, attracting oppressing remarks and behaviour not only from those who would be considered the stereotypical bullying type, but also from peers younger and older alike who would not ordinarily be the sort of people to comport themselves in such a manner. But for the fact that I experienced demeanour at their hands, they would otherwise have been decent people. I thought about committing suicide on a number of occasions.

For me, one of the most annoying things that well meaning (but in my opinion misguided) individuals say to those who worry about how to get other people to like them are those vexatious words 'be yourself'. I tried being myself for many years and that never generated much affinity with my peers.

Despite the fact that the people in my life nowadays are more pleasant and I now have a formal diagnosis, my low self-esteem remains. Having been instilled into me over a very long period, it is not going to disappear overnight. On a more positive note, life has generally been much better for me as an adult than it ever was previously. My teenage years were definitely the worst days of my life, and thankfully those times are now behind me.

What strategies would you recommend to other adult Aspies to stay mentally well?

This is difficult for me to answer, as I am not the best authority on this topic (especially considering my answer to the previous question!). Given that I am supposed to be providing information based upon my own experiences, I will say what I can, although others may not agree with everything I say.

I could be venturing into contentious subject matter for some by mentioning antidepressants, but I do feel that taking such medication has helped me through a difficult period. I was prescribed a non-addictive antidepressant by my doctor, which I sought as a last resort following a period of feeling extremely dejected. Fortunately, they did help me to feel better. I have heard accounts from other people with Asperger's syndrome that antidepressants and some other kinds of medication have only served to make them feel worse, so any decision to use them should be taken with care. Everybody is different and what works for some may not work for others.

Secondly, avoid situations that you feel uncomfortable with, and don't try to force yourself or let others force you into doing something that you don't want to do. I have found that there are some things that I will just never be able to cope with, and if I force myself into doing these things in the hope that I will get used to it or learn to manage, I only become stressed and anxious. For me, a busy restaurant or pub would be the prime example. The combination of noise, food and socialising is something that I find unbearable, so most of the time I avoid these places.

Finally, a few things that I have found to be beneficial to my mental wellbeing: Fish oil and/or multivitamin supplements, owning a cat, and those foam ear plugs that you can buy in the chemist can be extremely useful in certain situations!

Please outline the attributes your individual expression of AS which you find positive?

When I was asked if I would write about my experiences of Asperger's syndrome with a view to providing useful insight and advice for others, my first thoughts were that I was the sort of person who should be taking advice, not giving it.

I have always tended to view life in a somewhat despondent light, and I struggle to focus on the positive aspects. I can't really concur with the sentiments expressed by some people that Asperger's syndrome is a 'gift', as for me, the negative aspects outweigh the positives. So far, all of the books that I have read by authors with Asperger's syndrome tend to overshadow the negative aspects by highlighting the positive, and express a view that having Asperger's syndrome is a good thing. Whilst I am very happy for those who are able to think about their Asperger's syndrome in such a way, it can be a bit depressing for those of us who are unable to share in those sentiments when we are constantly reading and hearing accounts of how others view their Asperger's syndrome as a gift. I would hope that other people who feel the same way that I do will gain some solace from merely knowing that they are not the only ones who do not like having Asperger's syndrome.

In any case, I do have some ideas about positive attributes. I believe that people with Asperger's syndrome have very strong morals, and a very highly developed sense of what is right and what is wrong. We are incensed by the injustices that exist in this world. Whatever the experts may say about persons with Asperger's syndrome lacking empathy, I believe that the majority of us are of an altruistic disposition, even if we don't always know how to show it. It upsets me to see any living thing suffer.

I have always been indifferent to peer pressure. Clothing is a good example. I am not easily influenced by trends and fashions, and if I choose to wear a particular item of clothing, I do so because I like it, not because it is fashionable. I also couldn't care less if something I am wearing is considered 'uncool' by anyone else. If I like it, I will wear it. So why do I consider this positive? Because it doesn't simply extend to matters such as what one wears. Take illegal drugs and tobacco, for instance. What is the point? Why do so many people willingly ingest these pernicious substances? Everyone is educated in school that these substances are harmful. We are told that consuming them is likely to lead to adverse consequences, and could possibly even result in death. Everybody knows this. So why do people smoke and take drugs, for goodness sake? I certainly can't understand why. It seems that neurotypicals do understand why. If having Asperger's syndrome means that I neither understand nor want any part in this peculiar aspect of society, that is definitely a positive thing in my mind!

Please outline (as briefly as possible!) your vision for AS adults in the future?

I am sure that the first thing that would come into the minds of many people with Asperger's syndrome when they are asked this question is that they would like greater awareness and understanding of the condition from the general population, and my ideas are no different.

In considering this question, I would like to draw a comparison to another condition - dyslexia. Dyslexics have achieved the recognition that they deserve. At one time, dyslexic people were perceived as being stupid or deliberately awkward. Thankfully, there are now significant resources and support available for dyslexics. Because of education and publicity, most of the population now has at least a basic understanding of what it means to be dyslexic. Dyslexia is no longer perceived as an illness, and there is no stigma associated with the condition.

Sadly, I feel that this is not yet the case with Asperger's syndrome. Considering what I sometimes see in the media, I feel that many people perceive us to be vacuous and disconnected. I think we need to reverse this unbalanced perception with a view to attaining the same recognition and understanding that people with dyslexia now enjoy.

I would also like there to be better knowledge and understanding from employers. It is ironic that the majority of people with Asperger's syndrome are hard working by nature, yet many experience difficulties when it comes to gaining and retaining suitable employment. This is certainly not because of inability. I am fortunate to have experienced few difficulties in this area, but this is not the case for everyone.

I understand that some architectural firms like to employ people with dyslexia, because dyslexics possess spatial awareness and lateral thinking abilities. People with Asperger's syndrome also possess many faculties that should be desirable to employers, such as attention to detail and the desire to carry out jobs to a high standard. I would hope that if greater awareness and understanding can be spread to employers, there will come a day when some of them will consider Asperger's syndrome to be a positive attribute in individuals who apply for certain types of job.

Please offer from your own experience your three top tips for other Aspies for getting the best out of themselves in adulthood?

1. Number one tip from me is to be physically active and keep yourself fit. I am aware that this idea will be particularly unappealing to some people, so I can only provide encouragement by talking about my own experiences.

   At one time, I used to be overweight. I was unfit and did little exercise. Fortunately I managed to change that, and I am glad that I did because I feel so much better for it.

   I feel that I was hugely let down by the schooling system when it came to physical education. I absolutely hated the subject. The compulsory ball games, team sports and athletics that were inflicted upon me were things that I was absolutely useless at, and as a result I detested them. My school never offered anything in this area that was productive for me. These experiences could easily have put me off from engaging in any physical activity for the rest of my life.

   I am pleased however to have discovered as an adult that there are some kinds of physical activity that are suited to individuals with Asperger's syndrome, and it is possible for anyone to find an activity that he or she enjoys and can become good at. In my case, I found enjoyment in cycling and attending certain fitness classes at the local leisure centre. Even if you consider yourself to be unfit and lazy, it is possible to change that. I know, because I did.

2. It will certainly be the case that your main area of interest will provide enjoyment to you, but depending on what that interest is, it may not be conducive to any sense of achievement – especially if your interest is, for example, something like playing computer games.

   If this is the case for you, try to find an additional interest or activity that provides both pleasure AND gives you a sense of achievement at the same time. This could be studying for a specific qualification in an area that interests you, developing your fitness, or even participating in a fundraising challenge for charity.

3. In this life, no matter what you are good at and no matter what you like doing, there are bound to be other people who can do things

better. There will always be others who can run faster than you, draw better pictures, are better chess players, better musicians, better photographers, can bake a better cake (!) etc.

Don't compare your abilities with those of others. If you do, it is all too easy to become disheartened and feel like a failure. Focus on things that you are good at and set yourself your own individual targets that are realistic for you and you alone. That way, you will better yourself and feel good about it.

Case Study 8

Name: Prefers to remain anonymous

Age: 34

Age diagnosed with Asperger's syndrome (AS): 32

Are you formally or self-diagnosed: Formally

As an adult, do you agree that the condition is a disability/disorder?

That's a difficult question. I think the answer depends on whom you ask. For one person the dictionary definitions may be a perfect description, whilst for someone else they may bear little relevancy. Personally, Asperger's syndrome is just a part of my personality and character, and, although it can make everyday things difficult sometimes, I get on pretty well mostly. Taken at face value, the words 'disorder' and 'disability' have very negative implications, but AS has positive points too and describing it in these very rigid terms is perhaps doing it an injustice.

Would you say that your mental health has suffered as an Aspie?

I would say that my mental health suffered mostly from not knowing that I was an Aspie. For much of the first 32 years of my life I realised that something was wrong – why did I feel so different from, and act so differently to, everyone else? If I had been diagnosed at a much earlier age then things may have been better, although of course this is impossible to tell with any great certainty. Society, such as it is, dislikes differences, even more so ones that can't readily be explained, and so even if I had been diagnosed earlier, AS may have just been seen as an excuse for poor behaviour early on in life and just plain weirdness later on. At school I was confused and insecure about my own behaviour and thoughts; at work I was frightened by them. My confusion and insecurity at not understanding my own behaviour led to a deep depression and thoughts of suicide which lasted, on and off, for many years. However, perhaps even more terrifying, was not being able to express to anyone how I felt. I could be in the depths of despair and still look and sound relatively normal, even cheerful. How could anyone who looks so cheerful most of the time be suicidal? Who would believe them? Nobody, I guess. As for the present, having only recently been diagnosed, I may still be in the 'honeymoon' period of relief for the much-needed explanations of the previous decades, but my mental health has never been better. Things are so much clearer now.

What strategies would you recommend to other adult Aspies to stay mentally well?

1. Find a support group or website and talk to other Aspies. Sharing your experiences with other people who understand your issues is the number one strategy I can think of. There are lots of Aspie websites on the Internet such as Aspie Village at http://www.aspievillage.org.uk where you can talk to and meet other Aspies. The Internet is also a good place for finding local support groups.

2. Be yourself, but be flexible. I think this is a great strategy, but sounds so simple that it hardly sounds like a strategy at all. Being yourself doesn't necessarily mean that you can't be flexible in your approach to social or other situations, just don't try constantly to be the person that you wish you were instead of the person that you actually are – I have tried it and it doesn't work. You end up having two personalities – the one that you are consciously trying to imitate, and the one that you revert back to when you are not thinking about it. It looks odd to people and it's ultimately futile because you will never quite manage it without a conscious effort all the time. As trite as it may sound, learn to be happy with who you are, and if you can't do that, just don't think about it.

3. Again, hardly a strategy, but a great trick I have learned to help out when I am low, is to take a perfectly normal day when you are feeling happy and relaxed and then mentally store it. Think about your life and circumstances at that moment, and then mentally lock them away in your brain somewhere. Remember exactly how you are feeling at that moment. Do it often – this is key, but only when you are feeling well. Do it at work when your boss has just praised you. Do it at home when you're sitting in a sunbeam and you're perfectly happy being alone. Do it when you're on the train dozing, daydreaming or looking out the window at the wonderful countryside rushing past. Do it in your place of worship when you feel God's presence. Do it anywhere, but make sure you put these memories away somewhere secure but easily accessible so that you can remember them at the drop of a hat. Then, and here's the clever part, when you are in a similar situation but not feeling so good, remember the moment when you were doing exactly the same thing but feeling happy. If your boss has just shouted at you, remember the time when you were in exactly the same position but your boss was praising you. (And remember that he or she is probably having a bad day too and

they're not still going to be mad at you the next time they see you. As an Aspie, you'll remember it much longer than they will.) If you're feeling lonely, remember the time when you were on your own previously but feeling happy. If your faith is at a low ebb, remember the way you felt when you knew that God was right there with you. It may all sound too simple to work, but it does work – if you let it.

Please outline the attributes your individual expression of AS which you find positive

Although I can be a little bit blunt sometimes, I can be very diplomatic too and can read situations very well. I am often asked to judge arguments between people or to take a balanced view of things at work. This is good and it makes me happy to be able to do this so well. I don't know whether this is a common trait among Aspies, or perhaps just something I've subconsciously learned to do, but whichever, it is a useful skill.

I am very good at my job, which, as far as my work colleagues are concerned, makes up for my clumsiness, forgetfulness and general weirdness. I am respected by them and I'm often quizzed about things technical. The IT work that I do can be very intricate and detailed which makes it absolutely ideal for someone like me whose brain works in fine details. It also means I can squirrel myself away in a room for hours at a time and not be disturbed by anyone.

Fashions, politics and coolness don't really bother me. I sometimes go to work looking a bit scruffy, and at weekends I can often be mistaken for a tramp. This probably bothers other people a lot more than it bothers me but it saves me money on luxuries like clothes. I have an ancient car, which, although very reliable, is pretty decrepit; if people just replace their car for fashion and to be seen to be cool then I consider myself lucky for not caring less. I think this is a very good thing and I like being like that.

I love being on my own; being on your own is a very cheap hobby to have. I have a den at home where I spend hours at a time sorting electronic components, service manuals and other stuff into various different orders. I also spend a lot of time fixing old televisions (my special interest), building little electronic gadgets, playing with my PC or listening to talking books. It's a small room in the quietest part of the house and it feels safe and warm. I love sitting in there in my comfy old leather chair, sometimes just listening to the rain against the window or to the trains rumbling past at the back of the house or watching the people outside.

Please outline (as briefly as possible!) your vision for AS adults in the future?

Personally, I think the future has never looked brighter for Aspies. With a lot more media coverage and general understanding of the condition, I think that the things that mark Aspies out as being different from other people are tolerated (or even appreciated) to a much greater degree than in the past.

Please offer from your own experience your three top tips for other Aspies for getting the best out of themselves in adulthood?

1. Inform your boss and colleagues about your condition and tell them how it can affect you in ways that may often be difficult for them to understand. If it difficult for you to communicate this by talking to them, just let your boss know that you have a problem which you would like to tell them about, but that you have difficulty explaining it face to face. Tell them that you would like to write them a letter or note explaining the main points of the problem. After they have read it, if they then want to know more about specific details, ask them to write the questions down. Also, find a good AS website that you are happy with, and point them toward it. Explain that many websites describe Asperger's syndrome with regard to children and so are probably not entirely relevant to your situation. If you are embarrassed talking about AS to your colleagues, ask your boss to explain your problems to them instead.

2. If you are distracted by noise, buy several sets of high-quality earplugs and scatter them liberally. Keep a pair with you at all times, put some at work, keep some at home, keep some at your auntie's house or wherever it is that you are likely to go. If you are bothered by the general chitter-chatter of colleagues or other noise at work, slip the ear plugs in and it's like you're in a different world. Make sure that you use good-quality plugs and that you know how to insert them correctly. If you work with a computer, have a technician adjust the monitor refresh rate (how often the picture is updated on the screen). Make sure it's as high as it will go. You may not notice that your screen was flickering before, but it can cause headaches, tiredness and sensory overload without you really knowing why. Once you have used a monitor with a high refresh-rate, you will instantly notice how flickery everybody else's monitors are and you'll wonder how you ever managed before. Newer type flat-screen (LCD) monitors don't suffer in the same way as the old fashioned kind, so if you can acquire one of these then so much the better.

3. If you are feeling overwhelmed by people or noise or if you are in a strange place, pretend you are back at home or in a quiet safe place and that you are just watching through a remote control system. If you are in a noisy railway station and there are suddenly hundreds of people rushing about, use your pretend remote control to guide yourself to wherever it is that you need to be. Find an object in the middle distance just above the heads of the crowd and stare at it. Don't worry about not looking where you are going – providing you are not looking straight up then your peripheral vision will provide enough information for you to avoid banging into oncoming strangers or walking off the edge of the platform. Don't switch back to manual control until you have arrived at your destination. Do this with conviction and it will work for you. It is what I do whenever I go anywhere where I'm not comfortable and for me it is a very good method of survival.

Useful Contacts and Ways Forward

The Missing Link Support Services Ltd.

For Individuals

Counselling, psychotherapy, diagnosis, social group, assessment social skills, specific individual support, advocacy, employment support

For Professionals

Training, consultation, workshops

For Carers

Training, consultation, counselling, individual support

Contact

www.missinglinksupportservice.co.uk
Email: vicky@missinglinksupportservice.co.uk
genevieve@missinglinksupportservice.co.uk

Asperger's syndrome Websites

Discussion forums, chat rooms, real life meet-ups for AS adults in the UK and Ireland

Aspie Village

www.aspievillage.org.uk

AspieTalk

www.aspietalk.co.uk

Mental Health Contacts

UK

Samaritans
Support for depressed, upset, anxious, confused, or suicidal individuals in the UK
Telephone: 08457 909090 (low cost call)
Saneline
UK Mental Health Helpline
Tel: 0845 7678000

NHS Direct
Support from trained nurses
0845 46 47

Republic Of Ireland

Samaritans
1850 609090

USA

The National Suicide Prevention Lifeline
24 hours a day, toll free
Tel: 1-800-273-TALK (8255)

Australia

Samaritans
Tel: 08 93 81 5555